Stuttering Superhero

Adventure #2
Melissa Meets her Stamily

By Kim Block

Illustrated by Cheryl Cameron

This book is dedicated to all those people who volunteered, and who continue to volunteer, in the stuttering community. It is because of all of your work that you have created a community for us to come to home to.

Special thanks to the Canadian Stuttering Association and the National Stuttering Assocation for playing a big role in my journey.

Canadian Stuttering Association   www.stutter.ca
National Stuttering Association   www.westutter.org

ISBN
978-1-775007-1-2-8

Melissa was a stuttering superhero who lived in Burnaby, BC. She wasn't afraid to stutter, and she taught other people about stuttering. It wasn't always easy, but she was brave.

In her first adventure Melissa discovered her freeze power.

Now Melissa was flying through the air. She was flying faster than a car or a train. Children on the ground gathered and pointed in the air.

It's a bird... It's a plane... Yup, It's a plane and Melissa's in it!

Melissa and her Mom were flying to meet other people who stutter for three days in Toronto, Ontario, Canada.

Her Mom called it a learning party. Melissa was excited and also nervous. She was going to meet other kids who all had at least one thing in common: stuttering.

Melissa wondered if they were all exactly the same.

Did they all have the same hair?

Were they all the same height?

What if they all showed up in the same outfit?

Melissa and her Mom entered the beautiful and very fancy Alexandria Hotel where the three- day learning party was going to be. "I feel like a queen coming here," Melissa beamed.

"There used to be a King who stuttered and they made a movie about him," Mom told Melissa with a smile.

After settling into their hotel room, Melissa and her Mom joined others in the family area.

"H-H-Hello, my name is Mary Woodly and I am the l-leader for the next three days. Come on in and m-m-meet the other children," Mrs. Woodly said. She was welcoming everyone who entered the room.

Melissa joined the rest of the children in the group. She loved listening as Mrs. Woodly explained the game they were going to play. Her stuttering was beautiful. Melissa just wanted to hug her.

Melissa met many other new friends at the learning party.

At lunch time they all sat together.

"I don't like st-stuttering," whispered Tal. "I feel like I am st-stuck in m----ud."

"It's ok to not like it," Melissa stated loudly.

"Sometimes I don't like it either. B-but we can be stuck in mud to-to-together. We'll splash in the m-mud, have a mud fight and roll like p---igs. Hating mud will not make it go away. You'll just be unhappy s-s-sitting in mud," said Melissa smiling.

Tal wrinkled his face.

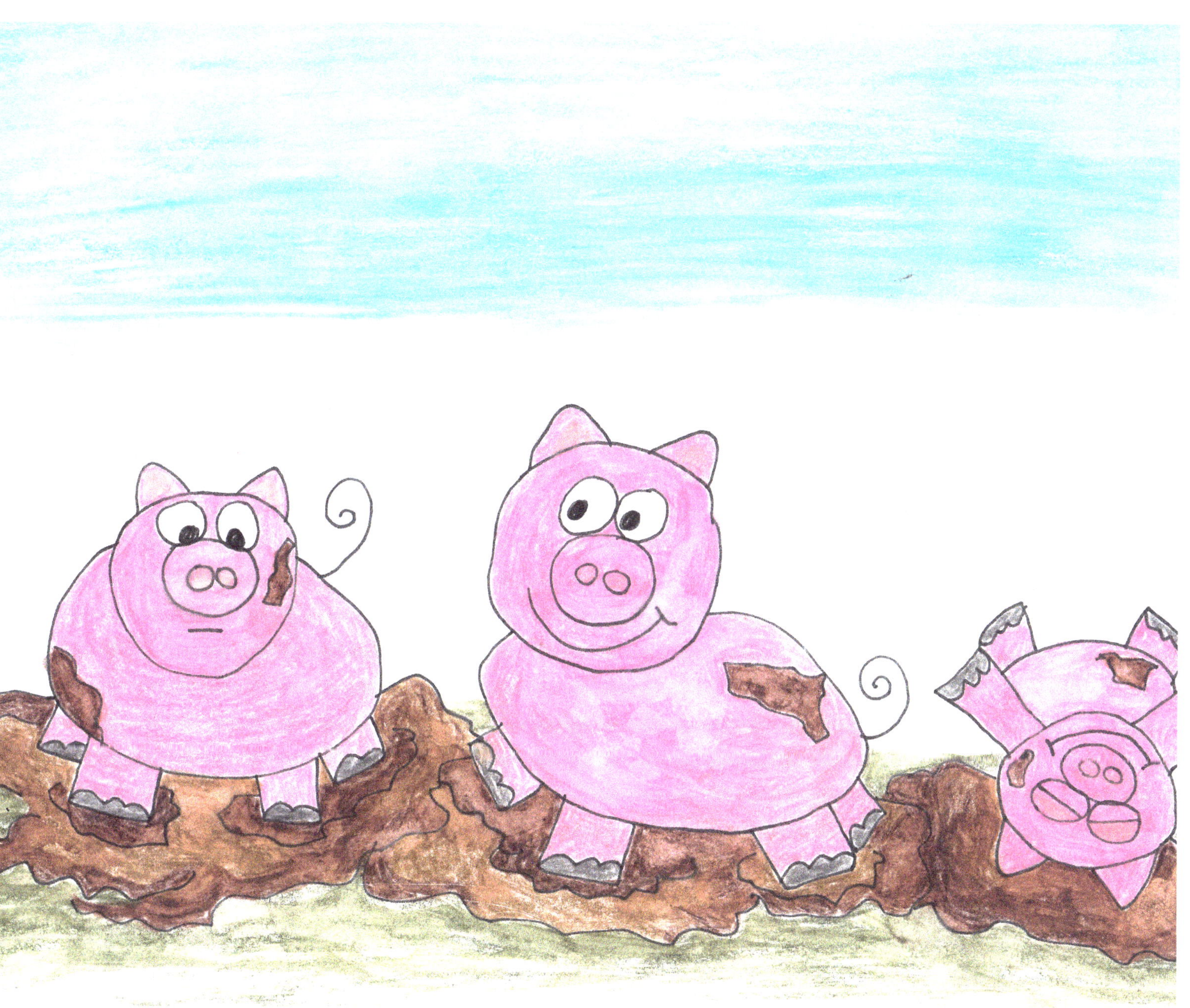

"I met a NASA rocket scientist, a nurse, a veterinarian and a teacher. They all stutter! So cool!" reported Jean-Paul.

"Wow, how-how do they do that?" asked Nancy. "Aren't they af-f-fraid to talk?" she wondered.

Mrs. Woodly was joining the group when she heard Nancy's question. "They are brave, they are strong, and they know when to ask for help. We never become who we are alone. When you are b-brave you help others feel brave," said Mrs. Woodly smiling.

"How do you find br--aveness?", asked Nancy.

"We all have it, every single person. Some days it hides and some days it shines. Being brave when you feel different means you are showing people it's ok to be you. We all feel different in some way. It doesn't matter the colour of your skin, the food we eat at home or the different clothes we wear. We all have the same heart," Mrs. Woodly said before she took a bite of her hummus and veggie sandwich.

Melissa spent the next three days playing in the huge pool, enjoying fun games and learning about how to teach others about stuttering.

Her Mom was busy talking to other adults who stutter too. She had a lot of questions and was always writing things down in a notebook. Melissa was having so much fun with her new friends Nancy, Jean-Paul and Tal. No one was afraid to talk and they weren't worried that someone was going to make fun of them.

Melissa felt free as a bird flying through the open sky. It was the best time of her life.

Melissa really liked talking to Mrs. Woodly and she thought she was very wise.

Melissa thought Mrs. Woodly must have x-ray vision. How could Mrs. Woodly read her mind and know what she was feeling, Melissa wondered.

"Wow, do I get these superpowers when I am older"? Melissa asked.

Mrs. Woodly smiled. "I re-remember what it was like growing up."

"All of us here are part of the stuttering community and we have so much in common we feel like we are family. You have met your stuttering family (st-amily) on this t---rip and these new friendships will last a lifetime. There is something so special when you look into someone else's eyes, f-f-feel in your heart that you are understood, and say the words "m-m-me too".

www.ingramcontent.com/pod-product-compliance
Lightning Source LLC
Chambersburg PA
CBHW040906070726
47599CB00038B/2330

Olivia Montuschi

Olivia Montuschi is the mother of two donor conceived adults, born in 1983 and 1986. She and her husband Walter Merricks founded the Donor Conception Network with four other families in 1993. Olivia trained as a teacher and a counsellor and for many years worked as a parenting educator and trainer, writing materials and running parenting education programmes. She now works part-time as Practice Consultant to DC Network.

Jane Ellis

Jane together with her partner Colin are the parents of two adult sons born through anonymous sperm donation. Jane is now retired from a career as a social worker, latterly in adoption and fostering, and as a counsellor for Relate. Jane joined the Donor Conception Network from its inception in 1993, and was a Trustee for many years. She and Olivia developed the DCN's Preparing for Parenthood and Telling & Talking workshops, for which Jane is currently the workshop manager. Jane also worked for a number of years for the Donor Conceived Register and the HFEA as a counsellor for donor-conceived adults, parents and donors.

Contents

Acknowledgments and Thanks

This is the last Telling and Talking booklet that I will be writing and maybe it is the last one that needs starting from scratch, although they all will continue to be updated regularly.

This booklet has had a longer gestation time than most, partly because I wanted to interview a large cross section of donor conceived young people, partly because it covers a longer period than the others but also because I moved house during the research! Lockdown during the Covid 19 pandemic has, however, proved the ideal time for writing.

First and foremost, enormous thanks go to the many teenagers and young adults whose thoughts and feelings on being a donor conceived person are at the heart of this booklet. I cannot thank you enough for your time and invaluable contributions. Thanks also to the parents I spoke to as well. Your love and concern for the well-being of your children was heart-warming to hear.

I am massively indebted to my long-time colleague Jane Ellis who has commented on and contributed to each chapter as it was produced. The booklet is written in my 'voice' because I conducted the interviews with the young people and parents. However, Jane's name appears as a co-author because her insights and additions have added immeasurably to the depth of the content.

Thanks also to Caroline Spencer, Ruth Yudkin and Lucia Grounds for your help with the chapter on Solo Mum and Lesbian Families.

And last but absolutely not least, thanks to my wonderful colleagues in the DCN office. Nina, Jo, Yael and Frances have kept my eye on the ball and occasionally my nose to the grindstone when I was faltering in my motivation. You are a great bunch.

Olivia Montuschi

July 2020

Continuing the Conversation:

A Guide for Parents of Donor Conceived Young People
and Adults from 12yrs Up

"I've always known about being donor conceived and felt really comfortable with it…but as I have grown older I have become more curious about genetic relatives, particularly half-siblings". Kate, donor conceived adult age 26

Introduction

Who is this book for?

Welcome to this addition to DC Network's series of booklets for parents of donor conceived people. It is aimed at parents who have been open with their children about their beginnings from an early age – but who are now wondering what the teenage and young adult years might bring. It attempts to be as inclusive as possible of all family and donation types and offer guidance that is useful for everyone. If you have not yet told your child about their beginnings by donor conception then one of the other Telling and Talking books will be right for you.

I suggest you read this first section and then pick and choose other chapters as they feel appropriate to your life and your questions.

What's in this book?

Our aim is to inform and guide you in supporting your child as they grow into a young adult. This is a time of life when young people's thinking about being donor conceived can shift…and shift again. They might become more curious about their origins and perhaps want to know more about DNA testing and its implications. I look at the increasing use of DNA testing to find genetic relatives and the use of the internet as a search tool or for peer support. Those young people conceived in the UK after 2005 might want to prepare for receiving information about the donor from the Human Fertilisation and Embryology Authority (HFEA). And you may want to get ready too.

Many parents of older children find they have very mixed feelings about what the teenage and young adult years may bring in relation to donor conception. There is discussion about this and information about the expected developmental stages which may help to put some of your child's behaviour into a wider context. There are suggestions on where parents and young people can find further sources of information, support and counselling.

How the evidence for this booklet has been gathered

I wanted this book to be reflective of the lived experience of today's donor conceived young people and their families. To this end I have interviewed 21 teenagers and young adults, plus my own adult children and 11 parents. Most of them (but not all) are members of DC Network.

As one of the founders of DC Network I have had (at July 2020) 27 years experience of talking with parents, children, young people, donor conceived adults and sometimes donors about their thoughts and feelings. I have 37 years of being a parent of two donor conceived people. I am also a member of four Facebook groups set up for donor conceived people, their siblings, donors and parents, of all donation and family types, where a whole spectrum of feelings about donor conception and being donor conceived are aired. Information about these groups will be given in the Resources section at the end.

Jane Ellis is a parent of two adult donor conceived sons; she is the manager of the DCN workshops and her additional experience of talking with donor conceived adults who have sought counselling via the HFEA register or the Donor Conceived Register makes her uniquely qualified to join me in the writing of this booklet.

Why is this book important and relevant for me as a parent?

In these pages you will find an exploration of the stages that teenagers and young adults go through towards forming their own identity. It's well known that teenage and young adult years can be confusing and difficult at times for all young people and their parents; the additional issue for donor conceived young people is that they have genes from one and possibly two other people to take into account.

None of us can know for sure how our children are going to feel about donor conception as they develop. Some young people never show any interest in their genetic relatives. However, the stories of many donor conceived adults who are curious show that parental attitudes towards this interest influence them greatly. If their parents seem reluctant and uncomfortable to talk about the subject, the young person is much more likely to keep their feelings to themselves. They may decide it doesn't feel safe to mention they are taking a DNA test or searching on the internet or even that they have curiosity about genetic relatives at all.

Of course, teenagers are notorious for becoming generally secretive, but a parent's chances of keeping a conversation going on this topic are much greater if their child has experienced a high level of support and openness over the years.

The family that your child has been raised in will of course have an impact on your child in a variety of ways. If yours is a solo, lesbian or gay household, you may have ensured you have built in extra resilience for your young child to answer such questions as 'if you don't have a dad/mum then how were you made?'. But the issue can raise its head again in early teenage years as young people often want to be 'normal' and just like their friends. Feelings can become more complicated in these sensitive years and at this time teenagers in solo mum or same sex couple families can sometimes wish that their family situation was more conventional. These feelings can change and change again as the years pass.

Over the years I have, together with my husband, worked with a number of older parents to help them prepare to tell their adult children for the first time that they are donor conceived. Those parents who can understand their child's perspective and maintain an open conversation over the months and years after 'telling' seem to retain the love and respect of their children. Those parents who are only able to see it from their own point of view, are unable to accept the initial feelings of anger and mistrust from their child and shut down conversations they are uncomfortable with, often find their relationships become fractured.

Despite friends and other peers becoming important influences in teenage years, parents, genetically connected or not, are everyone's primal influence. Never forget how much difference your approach and attitude can make to your teenage and adult children's lives.

A good start to thinking about your child moving into puberty and adolescent years is to ask yourself how you are feeling now, and if you have a partner, how you are doing as a couple with regard to donor conception. Have you, separately and together, resolved any issues you may have had at the start of the process or along the way? If not, it is never too late to re-visit them and/or talk with a close family member or friend or possibly a counsellor. The more resolved you are in your own head and heart, the better you are likely to be able to tune in to your child's feelings and needs. Ask yourself where you are on the openness scale. Not everyone needs to know of course and each family will have its own boundaries about 'telling' but you might want to think about whether you bring up the topic of donor conception in conversation with your child from time to time. You may think it is up to your child to ask if they need a question answered, but it is more likely that a teenager or young adult will do this if you show them that it is a safe subject to talk about by raising it yourself sometimes.

Some DC families have additional differences to manage. Where children have physical or learning disabilities, or mental health difficulties, the fact of their donor conception can sometimes feel like a secondary matter. It may be that during your child's younger years you have let the matter of donor conception quietly recede into the background. It is worth re-assessing this decision from time to time as every DC person has the right to know their genetic heritage as they get older. It could of course be that you suspect that the donor(s) may have contributed to your child's disability or difficulties.

Other additional differences can occur in families of different cultures and faiths, where norms and expectations influence how open parents and young people feel able to be about donor conception. Everyone's situation is unique and we hope you will be able to take from this book the parts that are helpful for you. It's always worth remembering there are confidential sources of support available through DCN.

Developmental Stages

Living with teenagers can be one of the most exciting periods in a parent's life: the vitality and energy of a teenager is infectious. Many parents find that they enjoy the challenge and the stimulation of living with teenagers. It is fascinating to see your children growing into young people with separate views, hopes and ambitions. You may be able to accept the moods and angry outbursts as part of the whole 'mixed package' but you may also be anxious about how this time of great change may impact on your child's feelings about being donor conceived.

We know from our workshops for children aged 8 – 13 that some children, even at the older end, are not aware of the range of families who might use DC for family creation or that there may be other children 'out there' who share the same donor. Some of the younger children, whilst being very familiar with DC, only seem to have a hazy idea that most people do not need to use DC and that there is another way to make a baby. It is unlikely that your child would not know about sex and reproduction by 12 but it might be worth checking how much they know about the many ways in which families are created.

As illustrated above, children develop, and understand what they are being told, at different rates. When thinking about your children now it can be helpful to try and think about what teenage years were like for you and then about how much it is both the same and different so many years later. Some of the differences are that families are much more diverse than they used to be. Every school has children from solo parent families, and increasingly children from gay and lesbian families too. Different ways of forming families, including donor conception, are becoming much more accepted. Today's older teenagers are much more comfortable with different sexualities, although young teens may repeat homophobic or racist views and language they have picked up at home or from peers. But despite these changes, the insecurities within the search for identity of this age group remains similar to previous eras, and generalised anxiety about the future is probably much greater now than in many previous generations.

The search for their own identity, the 'Who am I?' question, is at the heart of the developmental tasks, the things that need to be achieved before maturity is reached, of adolescence and young adulthood. Everyone goes through this separation process in their own way. Young teenagers in particular face a huge tension between wanting to fit in with their peers and finding out who they are as individuals. Donor conception may or may not make an impact on this struggle at this stage. What is likely to make a difference is having parent(s) who are able to tune in and listen to the feelings behind words (or silences) and adjust their responses and behaviour appropriately. Teenagers and young people can be infuriating and there can be a temptation to distance yourself from their moods and constant changes of mind, but a well placed 'How are you doing?' and the focus and time to listen to the answer, can make all the difference at any age. Resist all attempts to 'fix them' – they can only fix themselves in their own good time, but being available when they need you – and that time is unlikely to be at your convenience – can make the difference between them managing their feelings…or not.

The biggest difference of course between your own teenage years and that of your children is the massive development of technology and the dominant presence of social media. Few teenagers feel that they cannot be part of whatever is going on online, their phones having become almost an extension of their anatomy. This level of connectivity brings with it mixed blessings. The pressures faced by today's young people, where they cannot escape – unless they dare to turn off – the pestering compulsion of social media, is a constant nagging challenge to that central task of becoming an individual and not just one of the herd. A family I know have a house rule about phones/tablets/laptops not being in anyone's bedroom at night (including parents). The teenagers moan but comply, perhaps recognising inside that escape for a few hours at night is a good idea…although they wouldn't dream of admitting it.

Developmental stages

Looking at the different stages young people go through on their way to adulthood can help parents to consider the next stage before it happens and think about the possible additional implications for a donor conceived young person. It can be helpful to remember that age in years is not necessarily the same as the developmental stage your child is at. All sorts of things can delay development in one of the three types shown below and it is quite normal for one of the growing processes to be out of sync with the others, e.g. the child who shoots up in height but remains emotionally much younger. It is useful to keep this in mind when helping your child to make sense of donor conception. Individual experiences contribute to your child's cognitive, social and emotional development so it is different for each child within a family.

The three stages of growth.

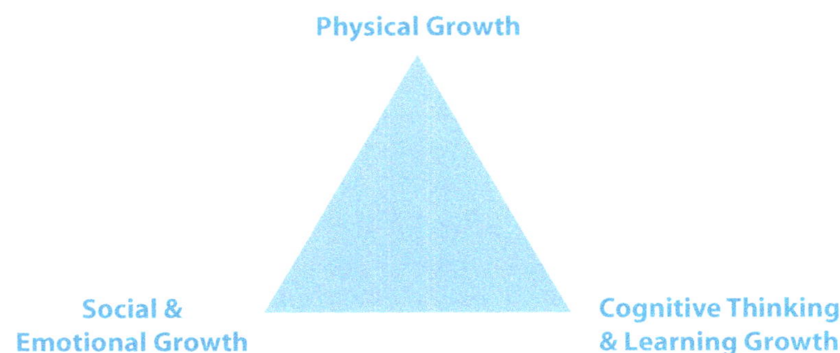

Younger Teens

At around twelve or thirteen noticeable changes are taking place in children's minds, bodies, emotions and behaviour. At this stage, pre-teens and young teenagers often make a push for independence but without the accompanying emotional maturity to manage the consequences. The brain, body and hormonal system are undergoing a complex combination of changes. Some young people may begin to think about what being donor conceived means for them, but for others it is the feelings that are aroused by the changes taking place in body and mind that are preoccupying them.

Although young teens might understand more of the facts and processes around DC, they may feel at a loss as to what to make of it all emotionally, and express anger or resentment at the parent who has presented them with this additional challenge. Teenagers often turn to friends for support but this may or may not be a topic they want to share with their own age group as 'fitting in' means a lot at this age. This is generally a difficult stage to keep communication going but it may be that a parent is the only person a young teen can talk to about DC, if something comes up for them. Remembering this and stepping back to consider the changes taking place in this age group can be helpful at this time when parents need to think before feeling provoked into being irritated or dismissive. It can help to get back in touch with your own early teenage years as a way of making it easier to empathise with your child.

Middle Teens

Middle-teen years tend to be dominated by the demands of school and exams on the one hand and concerns about friendships, developing sexuality and ever-present social media on the other. They may be thinking about whether they want to search for their donor(s) and/or genetic half-siblings and begin to realise the potential of the direct-to-consumer genetic testing companies. They may be preoccupied with the significance of genes and wonder what characteristics they have inherited from their donor(s). It is a very delicate balancing act for young people to manage and a time when donor conception may either disappear under layers of competing interests or alternatively become a dominant theme in a young person's developing sense of self. Appearance and attractiveness to others are all-important to this age group and so looking or not looking like other members of the family may or may not be a source of concern. Human beings are social animals and looking or being similar to emotionally close or admired family members is a way of identifying with a tribe. If a young person feels they can't identify in some way with close family this may trigger searching for someone who does look like them or has the same interests and talents.

Older Teens

Eighteen to twenty year olds will be moving out in to the world, possibly going into higher education or apprenticeships, travelling the world or seeking a first job. If things have gone pretty well in the family during the earlier teenage years they are likely now to be feeling confident in their knowledge of how they were conceived but perhaps not yet fully formed in their identity, which will develop further over the course of their twenties. So much is going on for young people at this time of life that those who are doing well emotionally may find that questions about donor conception are temporarily put to the back of their minds. Those whose teenage years were more of a struggle and perhaps whose parents have found more difficulty in accepting their growing child's feelings around being donor conceived, may be using their new independence to begin searching for genetic relatives.

Twenties and Thirties

Although young adults attain legal majority at age 18, most mental health professionals these days believe that emotional and social maturity is not really reached until around 25. By this time, if all has gone well, young adults will have largely achieved independence and autonomy from their parents and acquired a stable, well established personal and sexual identity. Brain development will of course continue for the rest of life, influenced by experiences and education.

At this stage in life thoughts turn to the possibility of the next girl/boyfriend being a life partner. Even if your adult child has not been making a habit of telling those they are in a relationship with that they are donor conceived or asking them if they are, this is a time when those forming couples might start doing so because of the risk of them unknowingly having an intimate relationship with someone genetically linked to them. Thoughts and feelings around being donor conceived are likely to become more nuanced but also clearer the older someone becomes. Independence of thought and action may release some twenty or thirty-somethings to follow avenues of interest in their genetic background that may not have felt possible or of interest before.

As children of early Network members move into their late twenties and thirties we are learning more about how their views have changed – or remained consistent – over the years.

> Our own daughter, now 34, has talked with her dad and me about not feeling she could speak openly on her feelings about being donor conceived when she was younger because we were so involved in DC Network. In fact her feelings were much more mixed than the image she conveyed when talking to the press, as she often did. Although it was painful to hear this, we are glad she felt able to tell us, but it was not until she was in her late twenties and much more sure of her identity. She and I took DNA tests when she was 30 but no relatives closer than third cousins appeared.

> Kate, 26, had always felt completely comfortable with being donor conceived but her curiosity about half-siblings and interest in her medical history grew as she became older and she finally took a DNA test. You can read about the result in the section on DNA testing.

> Sam, 28, also took a DNA test in the second half of his twenties. You can read more about his story later in the booklet.

Research into the needs of adopted people to find their birth families has shown that the interest really surges from twenty-five for women and about thirty plus for men. Entering into life-time relationships and having children are well known triggers for reflection on family connections and heritage. Becoming a parent has been the catalyst for some early-told sperm donor conceived adults to engage with regulators and governments as well as on forums for donor conceived people around policy issues to do with donor conception. We have heard from them that having a child made them realise how much they had missed by not knowing about, or indeed knowing in person, the man who had contributed to half their genetic make-up. On the other hand our son, now aged 37 and dad to two young children, remains as uninterested in his genetic background as he ever has been. My co-author Jane has one child who has always been interested in his beginnings by sperm donation and another who has never shown any interest at all.

Communication is key

Hopefully this chapter will have helped you to understand what might be going on for your child/young adult during these critical and often tricky stages of development. You may all sail through adolescence and young adulthood with few rough seas or you may have a more tumultuous ride. It is always difficult to know what part of the very natural ups and downs of this transition period are related to donor conception and what are not. Experience shows that most of the challenges facing our children are associated with the developmental tasks of the stage - essentially moving towards identity, autonomy and emotional stability. These, plus the changes in their bodies and brain development and the external demands of school, the exam system and of course the relentlessness of keeping up on social media. Ken Daniels, probably the foremost authority in the world on the dynamics of donor conception families, is clear that good communication between parents and children is the key factor in donor conceived young people being able to successfully negotiate these normal developmental tasks in full knowledge of their DC status. Participants in a study of DC adults conducted by Ken indicated that "relationships and communication within their families were of central importance in how they felt about themselves and their family."

Harriet, a 23 year old DC adult, told me that it was her mother's ease in talking about sex, relationships and emotions in general that helped her feel she could take any mixed feelings she had to her mum during what she described as 'the weird teenage years', because she knew she would be received with empathy and understanding.

I asked all the young people I interviewed what their advice to parents of teenagers and young adults would be. They all mentioned good communication in one way or another. Adam, age 17, probably summed it up best by saying –

"The way you discuss the topic will influence how your child feels about it. Treat them like an adult, offer options and LISTEN. Be ready for emotions. Make sure the focus is on their feelings and not on yours. Give your child a sense of freedom but keep a watchful eye."

Terminology

It is likely that you have always referred to the man or woman (or both) who contributed their eggs, sperm or embryos to help create your child as the 'donor(s)'. As children reach adolescence they may start to try out different language. Don't panic... as in so many areas, young people are trying out different ideas and ways of being. Teenagers, and indeed adults, can struggle with trying to find appropriate terms. Some young people come up for a while with 'real mum/dad'. They might say of the donor: 'Technically, that's my dad.' Or ask 'Does this mean you're not my real parent?' Although many parents dread this question, in DCN's experience it doesn't get voiced as often as you might think. Young people, no matter how they struggle with the language, are unlikely to see the issue as 'real parent' vs 'not real parent'. It helps a great deal to keep in mind that this question, however phrased, is not a personal attack, but part of your child's attempt to make sense of the information they have about being donor conceived. Generally young people are not looking for an alternative parent. One response to the use of the word 'real' could be something like:

'That's an interesting word to use, how did you get to make that connection?' The end result will be that the story gets re-shaped by the person who is ultimately going to own it.

You might be asked: 'What made you pick this donor?' Depending on your circumstances, you could talk about any personal statements or pen portraits, the fact that you trusted the doctor who made the match or personal characteristics of the donor. If you have more detailed information about your donor than you have given your child so far, this might be the time to ask your child if they want to know more right now. Those with known donors (particularly from within the family or a close friend), often ensure that their child knows about them, even if they don't understand the connection, from a young age. If you are in a heterosexual couple and have a known sperm donor, it is important to ensure your child is clear that their mum did not have sex with this person. It might also help to ensure that conversations about characteristics of the donor also includes looking at what traits your child shares with you as a result of you having spent time together whether you are the non-genetic or genetic parent.

Language around donor conception has always been a minefield as we struggle to find new words for new relationships or try to make old ones fit. You might like to think about the term 'donor'. We have historically attached 'the donor' to the child so that we refer to 'your donor' when talking to them. The truth is however, and this is borne out by the Morgan Centre research with gamete donors (see section on Donors) that the donor(s) gave his or her gametes or embryos to us so that we could become parents, so logically the donor is ours and not that of our child. Our donor(s) is actually our child's biological parent(s), so perhaps the word 'donor' isn't the right one to use. However, using the term 'biological parent' in a social context can feel unwieldy and formal so 'donor' feels like useful shorthand in many circumstances. Changing how we use the word 'donor' seems to be part of a movement away from euphemistic language and towards even greater clarity and openness about donor conception, led by some donor conceived adults. But there is no orthodoxy here. Whilst all of us need to think about the language we use, it is probably best to let your teenage or adult child find the terms they are happy to own, and remember that these may evolve over time.

Those young people who are interested in their beginnings and want to explore the terminology around donor conception may end up referring to the donor as their bio-dad or mum. But many will continue to use the term donor, sometimes inter-mingling it with other terminology, perhaps even a nickname, depending on the context. Whatever words are used by you or your child it is highly unlikely to be of real significance if the relationships and communication in the family are good, and if they are, then all is likely to be well.

Where surrogacy has been used, donor conception is almost inevitably part of the picture, unless an embryo created with the gametes of the intending parents has been used. In traditional surrogacy, the egg of the surrogate is fertilised with sperm from the intending father (so the surrogate is the egg donor). Gestational surrogacy usually involves a separate egg donor as well as a surrogate. The language used in surrogacy sometimes revolves around referring to the surrogate as the 'tummy-mummy' or alternatively using her first name to make it clear that mummy and daddy are the raising parents. In her interview with Canadian journalist Alison Motluk, 21 year old UK surrogate-born Gee Roberts talks about knowing from a young age that she had two parents but also her 'tum-mum.' She now sees her surrogate (who is also her genetic mother) as an "auntie-type figure" or close family friend.

As with other family types, the language you use to describe your surrogate and your egg donor is likely to change as your child grows. It might be that the egg donation part of the story has felt like a minor role compared with that of carrying and giving birth to the child, particularly if you have an on-going relationship with your surrogate. If your egg donor is not also the surrogate, both you and your child might find yourselves wondering about what traits and likenesses she might have contributed, and a discussion about the complexities of the roles of surrogate and egg donor might be helpful. You might want to revisit together with your child the place in your family life for both the surrogate and the egg donor as your child becomes old enough to have their own views.

School Matters

The transfer to secondary school is often a time of great anxiety for parents. Children these days are mostly very well prepared for the change but parents worry about moving from the intimacy of a small primary school where each individual child is known to teachers. Nearly all parents wonder if staff will notice if their child is being bullied or is failing to fit in. Channels of communication can be hard to fathom in large schools and parents often feel they are being held at arms length, whereas in primary school teachers were easily accessible. Parents of donor conceived children (as well as those who have children with a range of differences and disabilities) can worry that their child is being left on their own to manage something that they are still struggling to fully grasp for themselves.

For children from solo mum, lesbian or gay families it is often their family type that causes more comment than anything to do with donor conception and again causes anxiety for parents at the transfer to secondary school.

Raphy, nearly 18 at time of interview and conceived by sperm donation, said that having two mums was sometimes quite tricky to negotiate when he was younger and he had to do quite a lot of explaining. By contrast his half-sib Ruby from a heterosexual couple family, (and from the same sperm donor) could choose whether or not to mention being donor conceived. Maybe girls' schools are different, but Lucy, also conceived through sperm donation and from a two mum family, found that in her early teens her friends didn't really understand about DC, but now she is fifteen, having two mums and being DC is considered very cool. She even used donor conception as a practice topic for an exam.

Hopefully this section will give you some ideas about how you can best support your child, without disturbing their increasing need for independence.

Once your child reaches secondary age, it is likely that you will have largely handed over responsibility for the sharing of DC information with the school to your child/teenager. But in this time of transition young people often find it helpful to continue to share the responsibility with parents for a while. Young teenagers often don't want to discuss anything to do with donor conception anymore. Many are entering a phase where they want to keep anything personal to themselves and this often goes alongside finding parents intensely embarrassing. A casual conversation with your child before any occasion where the issue of donor conception could come up, like a doctor's appointment, could serve as a check on whether they want to share the information or would prefer the see-saw of responsibility to swing to you this time.

Modern secondary education offers many opportunities for debate on moral and ethical issues, often within the context of religious education or English classes. Sex and relationship education may or may not include anything about the different ways families are made, while biology lessons concentrate on facts rather than feelings.

From talking to young DC people it is clear that biology lessons in early teenage years have been a catalyst for further understanding of what it means to have been conceived with a donor/donors. A basic introduction to genetics could lead a child to understand for the first time what having a donor really means – no biological link, no DNA shared with one or both parents. Egg donor conceived Isabella only really understood the non-bio link at age about 12 or 13 although she was keen to tell me that this wasn't a big deal for her. Edward, also egg donor conceived, said that he didn't really understand until early teenage years. For some this can have a big impact: not only sadness but also an amplified feeling of difference. It might kickstart some thoughts about wanting to trace a donor and it might also dawn on some for the first time that they may have half-siblings out there somewhere. A young person born through gestational surrogacy might have additional confusion about having been gestated by another woman without sharing any of her DNA. Those born through embryo or double donation may feel they have more to grapple with as they have no genetic connection to their parent(s) and have two donors to consider.

At a time when teenagers are wanting to fit in with others, these new insights carry the potential for upset and are something parents will want to watch out for. Our son Will, then age about 14, found himself completely frozen when a homework assignment included writing an essay about assisted reproduction. He just couldn't write a word. With his permission we contacted the appropriate teacher, explained about Will's dilemma and she was able to excuse him that piece of work.

All of the above scenarios are ones that may come up for your child but the overwhelming evidence from experience within DC Network is that most teenagers seem to manage information about donor conception at school without it becoming a huge issue, either within themselves or with friends. Personality seems to be the major difference with the way young people handle it. Some will be happy to talk about being donor conceived in class because they quite enjoy being in the limelight. Others are more private people and see no reason to share this personal fact about their origins with their classmates. Most, however, seem to share the information with a few people they have developed trusting relationships with and leave it at that. No-one mentioned being bullied because they were donor conceived.

There is no evidence that there is any particular meaning to be attached to the different ways that children handle the information.

Sam, now 28, shared information about his conception with classmates in a PHSE (Personal, Health and Social Education) lesson when he was about 13 and enjoyed the attention he received (and the disruption of the lesson) as a result. He reported no comeback from this, but by the time he was 15 and realised he was gay, he stopped wanting to draw attention to anything different about himself.

Brothers Ben and Jamie have never mentioned their sperm donor conception at secondary school. Their parents had told every year teacher at primary school but did not continue this once their sons had moved on.

Egg donor conceived Edward has never felt the need to tell friends in school or outside about his conception.

Sperm donor conceived Harriet always found donor conception an interesting topic and told friends at school. They found the information 'dramatic' although Harriet herself thought it perfectly ordinary. Like Harriet, her older brother Ben told everyone at school. In a Religious Studies lesson where the topic touched on IVF and sperm donation, a classmate said, "That's what Ben's parents did". Ben was not bothered by this but for a more sensitive young person it could have been a problem.

Having been bullied in primary school (not about her origins) Ellie did not want to draw attention to herself in secondary school so told no-one. Now at university she would like to share her beginnings with new good friends, but still finds it difficult to know how to start the conversation.

It can be a good idea to discuss with your child before going to secondary school how they handle questions that might be tricky and who to tell or not, and check back in regularly when topics are raised at school that might be relevant. It is helpful if you can find out what the school curriculum contains at this stage, watch out for any difficulties your child may be having and consider whether or not they are related to the processing of new information about being DC. Most times they won't be but sometimes they will, so in addition to offering support and discussion at home you may want to talk with your child about whether it would be worthwhile (selectively and privately) to share some information with an appropriate teacher.

Unfortunately teacher sensitivity cannot necessarily be relied upon when addressing the topic of assisted conception in class as egg donor conceived Isabella found out. She is in Year 12 now but when she was younger and in a biology class where donor conception was mentioned, the teacher asked if anyone in the class was conceived that way!

It may be that your faith or cultural community do not have views aligned with your own about openness in donor conception and that these differences may cause confusion for both you and your child. The importance of blood lines and privacy for the family are also part of the culture in some ethnic communities. It will be imperative for parents from these communities to know what their child's school's official line on assisted reproduction is and be prepared to talk to children about any possible tensions between what is being taught in school, the culture they are being raised in and what they as parents believe.

Adam, 17 and at a Jewish secondary school, told good friends and was made to feel normal by a new GCSE Religious Studies curriculum where IVF and donor conception are talked about. Although this is a faith school, they follow a non-religious curriculum in this topic.

Katherine, who is in a lesbian partnership and the mother of Milly, wrote to the Network about how a discussion has been prompted in her household by a debate held at her daughter's school:

"It has been a significant time for Milly and us around 'telling' and feelings raised about being donor conceived. This was triggered by an ethical debate in GCSE Religion around methods of conception and becoming parents and 'multiple parentage' – gamete donation, surrogacy and legal parents. All quite heavy material for a 14 year old, especially one who has chosen to be so private about her donor conception as a teenager."

Identifiable, Known or Anonymous donor: Preparing your Child for the Future

If your child was conceived in the UK on or after April 2005 then the year 2023 may have a special significance for you. It is in this year that the very first people conceived with the help of an identifiable donor, will turn 18 and thus have the right to ask the HFEA for identifying details of the person or people who gave their sperm or eggs (or both) to help create them. In fact there may not actually be many in 2023, given the nine month gestation time, but they will increase from 2024 onwards. If you conceived abroad or in the UK before 2005 then your child will not have this opportunity to gain information. If you have a known donor, your child may or may not have had contact with their donor from birth. This chapter explores what these different scenarios may mean for you, your child and your family.

Identifiable at 18 donor

Over the years I have spoken to many parents about their feelings about their donor becoming identifiable to their child at 18. Most have believed that the 2005 law change was the right step to take so that their child(ren) could have a choice about contacting the donor, but their own feelings about it have varied enormously. A few, particularly some single women, wish that the identity of the donor and half-siblings could be made available earlier in a child's life so that their child could grow up knowing these people. Some people have chosen donors known to them personally ('known donors') for just this reason and others, again usually single women, have chosen sperm donors from American banks where early connections may be possible via the American based Donor Sibling Registry or increasingly a bank's own database.

Heterosexual couples tend to be the most ambivalent about the donor or half siblings becoming known to their adult child. They speculate whether these people will be family, complete strangers or something more aligned to distant relatives. It is true that donors and half-sibs will not share a genetic relationship with anyone other than the child or children whose conception they contributed to so everything will depend on the meaning that your child attaches to this genetic link. There is very little published about outcomes of meetings between donors and offspring but links to what there is are given in the Resources section. The great majority of these accounts refer to sperm donation. Online forums give some American and Australian accounts of very happy and successful meetings and on-going relationships, often including mum and dad as well, but there are also heart breaking stories of donors who do not respond or are cold and dismissive of their DC children. Outside of Victoria, Australia, where progressive legislation facilitates contact between genetic relatives, these are almost all stories about anonymous donors who have been traced via DNA testing or because their donor information has become identifying in the internet age. The UK situation is different because post 2005 donors will have been counselled about their responsibilities in eighteen years' time. See more on this topic in section on Donors later on in the booklet.

Sweden was the first country to end anonymity for donors but it is unusual in that the change was legislation-led and that openness with children did not follow to the extent legislators had hoped. The doctors were against it and there was no parent organisation, like DC Network, or donor conceived adults to take up the cause on behalf of the children. The truth is that after Victoria and probably New Zealand as well, the UK has led the way in openness and this means that there are potentially large numbers of post 2005 conceived young people who will be eligible to ask for donor information from 2023/4. They and their parents will be (possibly reluctant) pioneers in the exploration of making contact and seeing what happens next. In the section on Practicalities you will read that support will be available from the HFEA if your child wants to ask for identifying information, but your open-mindedness, flexibility and willingness to be there for your child whatever comes about will be highly valued.

There is more on this topic in the sections on Talking and Sharing Information and Meeting the Donor later in the booklet.

Families with known donors

It may be that those parents who have a known donor have a lot to teach about their experiences of integrating the donor into their family, so their stories can be interesting to search out. Here there is potential for family relationships to develop more organically, as agreed by both parties together. If this is your situation, you may feel yourself (perhaps not for the first time) to be a reluctant pioneer - there are no established guides or scripts to follow. You may have had to negotiate how relationships would be defined from very early on in family life. As your child is now approaching adolescence, or older, the dawning of realisation of what genetics actually means (as discussed in the chapter on schools) may have a particular resonance for them in the context of, say, a beloved 'auntie', who is actually their egg donor. Distinguishing 'social relationships' from 'genetic relationships' and defining the relative importance of each is a complex matter. It's not made any easier by the paucity of terms to describe these relationships, which may well be 'special' but don't seem to fit with either family or good friends terms. The relationship you negotiated when your child was born is very likely to change shape over time due to normal life events and increasingly from now on, the feelings and wishes of your child.

Thirteen year old Jacob, who spoke at a DC Network meeting when he was only 11, has two mums (who now live separately) and a known donor. When I asked Jacob about his relationship with his donor he said,

"My relationship with my donor, Richard, hasn't changed (since the meeting). I see him a few times a year when he comes to Bristol, and we usually spend time together with other members of my family. We often find odd jobs that need doing, or we might play a game, or go for a walk - all sorts of things. It's really just like a family friend, I suppose."

One of Jacob's mums told me that Jacob has a hard time articulating what the relationship is like because "it's not really *like* anything - if you see what I mean. It's just an easy, straightforward relationship with no expectations and no agendas."

What if you conceived abroad and your child is not on the HFEA register?

If this is your situation then you may find it hard to read about young people preparing to ask for information from the HFEA about their donor. But it is also possible that you are, wholly or partly, feeling relieved that information about the donor is not instantly available to your child at 18. You may or may not be pleased that DNA testing (see section on this topic) could be a way for your child to find genetic relatives if they choose to follow this path.

If your child has contact with UK donor conceived young people either in person or via the internet or seeks information from the HFEA, they may be upset or angry to discover that they do not have the same rights to information. You may have been talking to them over the years about the country where they were conceived and perhaps going on visits, following sports teams or even learning the language but it may be that as 18 approaches they still have feelings of disappointment about not being able to have ready access to information and potential contact if this is important to them.

The advice to you is in principle exactly the same as for the parents who conceived in the UK, so do keep reading the whole of this chapter. First of all, listen to and get to understand your own feelings and then listen to your child and take your cues from them. Offer them the opportunities to talk about how they feel and let them know it is OK for them to express negative or mixed feelings. If it is appropriate you could say how sad you are that the laws in the country where they were conceived do not a low them to have the information they want. You could add that you did not realise at the time of your treatment how much donor anonymity could impact on them and (if it is true) how much you wish you had stayed/could have stayed in the UK. Whatever it is, having a consistent and coherent story to tell your child with conviction will go a long way to helping your child understand the circumstances of their conception and adjust to ways of managing their feelings about it. Some parents can feel a level of guilt about having chosen an anonymous donor, without understanding the potential consequences, and try to compensate by telling their child 'how wanted' they are. We have learned from donor conceived adults that some do not like the emphasis being put on a child being 'so wanted' as they feel that this implies that a child has to be grateful for being brought into the world and that the means always justifies the end. We know from experience that many donor conceived people do like to think of themselves as 'sought after, much wanted children' but probably best to allow a young person to come to that conclusion themselves rather than potentially putting any pressure on them to feel this way.

Lucia, who has thirteen year old embryo donation boy/girl twins conceived in Spain, has been very open with her children from early on, despite only knowing her donor's ages and blood groups. The children have spent time speculating about their ethnicity and have swung from being very proud of being Spanish to wondering if this is their genetic heritage at all (not all donors in Spain are Spanish). Lucia has talked with the children about their desire to know more about their genetic background and as this became a more insistent need for her daughter, she agreed to her undergoing a DNA test. This revealed an ethnic heritage that her daughter is very excited about. The story is on-going.

Revisiting feelings about genes

This might be a time when both you and your children find yourselves visiting or re-visiting that whole complicated area of the importance of genes. It may not be an area that you've thought hard about since you first made your decision to use donated gametes. You may have thought then about all the other types of families flourishing without being connected through genetics - adoptive, fostering and step-families - and have felt settled in your own mind that lack of shared DNA is no bar to forming and maintaining deep, nourishing bonds. And by now you have good experience of bringing up your family on that assumption. And yet some DC young adults feel a strong need to search for a genetic parent, or half-siblings. You might wonder what it is that they are looking for; whether there is something lacking in their upbringing. You might be alarmed that the consequences of your child bringing genetic relatives into their lives will affect your family life too. Anonymous or identifiable donor(s), whilst acknowledged in your family story, have remained somewhat shadowy figures for the majority of parents. And yet for many, perhaps most parents, their donor continues to have a kind of presence. You might find yourself every now and again searching your child's face wondering whether certain features are shared with the donor, whether character traits, health issues or emerging talents have a genetic link with this person. Some people feel that the very situation of keeping the donor's identity hidden throughout a child's growing up perpetuates a sense of unease that cannot be resolved.

 For some parents, thinking about the donor as a real person threatens their 'right' to be a parent, and perhaps their notion of what a 'proper' family should be. Some people too, find emotions of grief and loss have been awakened. If this resonates with you, please be assured you are not the only parent who struggles with this. It may be helpful to talk it over with your partner if you are a couple, trusted friends or a counsellor. You don't have the ability to change this situation but being more conscious of your own emotional reactions can be very helpful in preparing for the future. In fact, your experience of working through some of these difficult feelings could be very useful; some teenagers also feel sad, or angry, or confused, and your parallel experience could allow you to be more empathetic. Difficult questions such as if and where the donor fits into your family life, their role in your child's life, how your child might relate to their donor kin, suddenly come to the fore when you think about the future. The idea of half-siblings may feel more straightforward, particularly for those who conceived using a UK recruited donor, as the HFEA stipulates that no more than 10 families may share the same donor. However, in theory that could mean 15 or more siblings (though the HFEA's statistics show this to be unlikely.) For families with one or two children, these numbers can feel overwhelming. For those who conceived in the UK but using sperm from a US or Danish sperm bank, the numbers of half-siblings worldwide may be very large indeed. The HFEA only has control of how many families in the UK receive a donor's sperm and sperm banks in these countries tend to sell throughout the world. It is extremely unlikely that large numbers of half siblings are something young people conceived through egg donation will have to worry about, wherever they were conceived.

All these feelings absolutely fall within a normal spectrum but it can be helpful to try to unpick them a bit. First of all, if things have gone pretty well in the family over a child's first 18 years with normal ups and downs, then your child is likely to be emotionally embedded in your family (what psychologists call securely attached) and not to be looking for someone to transfer their allegiance and affections to. As discussed earlier late teens are at a time of exploration of self but within a wider world, a continuation of the search for an individual identity that may not settle for another ten years or so. Wanting to know about the person who contributed half or all of their DNA is all about them and not about you. It rarely has anything to do with rejection and replacement but is all about adding knowledge that helps to build an identity they can feel comfortable with. Of course, not all donor conceived people feel the need to explore their genetic roots, but DC adults posting on on-line groups that are open to parents and donors as well as offspring (mixed groups), often talk about wanting and hoping for acceptance by their parents of their need for information about their genetic progenitors. Their parents who raise them are the people they love first and foremost and it is a source of sadness and sometimes anger if they seem not to understand this need, or want to support their children.

There is no evidence that DC people who want to have information about their donor and half-siblings are any more or less well-adjusted than anyone else. Everyone is different and DC adults just want to have their particular needs respected.

How does your child feel?

The best way of finding out how your child feels about the possibility, or not, of discovering who the donor is, is to ask them! Keeping up good communication is vital – if sometimes challenging – in teenage years, but offering regular opportunities to voice thoughts and feelings on DC as well as a whole range of other topics will hopefully give the message to your child that this is a subject you are comfortable talking about. Children can be very protective of parents and if your child senses that a parent or parents would prefer not to talk about the donor or half-siblings, then they may not raise the subject themselves. Nothing being said by your child does not mean that they are not thinking about it but it doesn't mean they are either. A few young people, mostly male I have to say, simply do not give the topic more than a passing thought, but the majority of donor conceived young people seem to have a curiosity that may wax and wane over the years.

Kate's curiosity about her donor and half-siblings, but mostly half-siblings, went up and down for years before she finally decided to take a DNA test age 25 (read about this in the section on DNA testing)

Ben, 17, is very curious about half-siblings but is aware that his younger brother is much more cautious. As they share a donor Ben is unlikely to make a move unless his brother decides to join him.

Teenagers I have spoken to who will have the right to the identity of their donor after 2023 have voiced a variety of views. These range from excitement to trepidation to disinterest to a feeling that they might wait a few more years before asking for the information. Eighteen year olds are right at the threshold of independent life. They may want to include exploration of genetic roots as part of finding themselves but they may also decide that this is not the right time to enquire after this particular bit of knowledge. Adoption studies have shown that of the percentage of adopted people who want to know more about birth parents, most do not get started until around 25 or so. Women tend to search earlier than men do. Some only want information; a smaller percentage are looking for contact as well. We cannot know how many donor conceived adults entitled to identifying information about their donor will want to take this up or when. You can only prepare yourselves and your children for whatever the future brings.

Those young people who do not have the right to identifiable information, either because they were conceived in the UK before 2005 or because they were conceived abroad, have spoken of a wide spectrum of feelings from frustration and/or anger to ambivalence or having been resigned to the situation for a long time.

Preparing yourselves and your child for 2023 and beyond

First of all, the practicalities. Although identifying information will be available from the Human Fertilisation and Embryology Authority (HFEA) on or after a young person's 18th birthday, quite a lot of information can be asked for by parents any time up until their child is 18 or by a young person themselves from age 16. It is worth remembering that this is information that was given by the donor 16 or 18 years ago and things may have changed since.

- The donor's physical description (height, weight, eye and hair colour) if provided
- The year and country of their birth
- Their ethnicity
- Whether they had any children, how many and their gender at time of donation
- Their marital status
- The medical tests that all donors are required to undergo
- A goodwill message to any potential children (if provided). (The HFEA will redact any information in this message that might reveal the donor's identity).

In addition, 16 year olds, like those conceived since 1991, can ask about the number of half-siblings conceived using the same donor, their gender and the years they were born. They can also enquire as to whether someone they are in a serious relationship with is also donor conceived (with that person's permission).

At 18 a young person can ask for:

- The donor's name
- Date of birth
- Last known address

They can also at 18 request to be added to the Donor Sibling Link register in order to be put in touch with half-siblings by mutual consent.

The HFEA recognises that young people from the age of 16 may have strong and/or mixed feelings about the prospect of asking for information about their donor. There is plenty of information on their website; in addition, counselling support is available to all those who would like to talk over their feelings and explore the implications of contacting their donor, or placing themselves on the Donor Sibling Link Register. The HFEA strongly encourage people to take this up, and will pass on a referral to an experienced external agency, who will then contact the young person directly. Up to five free confidential sessions are available to support them, either face to face or by phone or Skype to think through what they are hoping to get from the information they receive and how the process works. It also includes if requested a mediated face to face session with the DC person and their donor or half-sibling. The same service in preparation for contact is available for donors although of course they are not entitled to identifying information about any child en whose creation they contributed to.

How do the donors feel?

Eighteen years (or more) is a long time and it is impossible to know where donors will be in their life and their thinking after all this time. It is possible that a donor will have died by then but it is more likely that if they were single or childfree at the time of donation, they might now be partnered and have children in their family. Any and all of their experiences since they donated may have coloured their view about the commitment they made so many years ago. Hopefully most donors will be traceable and open at least to providing information about their and their family's health and background, but it is impossible to know in advance. It can also be hoped that most donors will have told their family about donating and about the possibility of young people seeking them out. Early identifiable donors may have a sense of being pioneers in the new openness about forming families by donor conception. They may be anticipating the time when contact will be made with interest. Others may have put that part of their life in a box and shut the lid. Only time (and good research) will tell us how these things pan out. What parents can do is help prepare young people for the range of scenarios they may encounter.

At the time of writing this booklet an interesting piece of research titled 'Curious Connections' is being written up by a team from the Morgan Centre for Research into Everyday Lives at the University of Manchester. They interviewed egg and sperm donors, both known donors and identity release donors. Identity release donors are men and women who donated through UK clinics and who will become identifiable when a donor conceived person turns 18. Their experiences were all different of course but a strong unifying factor was their moral sense of 'knowing their place', and acknowledging their recipients as 'the parents', and they often looked to the donor conceived family to lead the way in any on-going relationships because they did not want to seem imposing or interfering. Interestingly, they often felt an affinity with the recipients, even if they didn't know them. Leah Gilman, one of the researchers, reports in the leaflet 'Being an Egg or Sperm Donor: balancing 'being available' with 'knowing your place' (see Resources section) describing the findings of the project, that donors of all types were keen to stress a neutral morality epitomised by the following phrases:

"All on their terms"
"I would want them to be the creators of the parameters"
"I'm being very much led by them"
"Play it by ear"
"A hands off approach"
"It's got to be down to them"

All but one or two of the men and women interviewed had donated since 2005, when anonymity in the UK was removed. You may feel that their approach, as stated above, is good news. Donors don't see themselves as parents and are likely to take their lead from the donor conceived person when contact is made at 18 or probably before in the case of known donors. But, as Gilman acknowledges, being neutral in a relationship is a very odd way to behave and it will be interesting to know how these feelings pan out as children have thoughts and feelings of their own, connections are made and real relationships come into play.

At an event to publicise their findings, researchers drew out what they termed 'the moral tension' for donors, who want to signal their readiness to engage with their donor offspring should that be asked for, but at the same time are wary of being felt to encroach on parental roles. This came to the fore particularly for known donors, who were often family friends, and found themselves self-censoring comments which might have been perceived as parenting suggestions. Some donors found themselves to be in a quandary about whether to talk to their own children about the fact that they had half-siblings in one or more other families. Some of the questions donors asked themselves are echoed by many parents: who needs to know and why? You might be interested to know that in the UK donors' partners are encouraged by many clinic counsellors to participate fully in discussions about what donating gametes involves.

Details of the book that will emerge from this research can be found in the resources section at the end of the booklet.

Talking and sharing information

You may have already shared some of the non-identifying information with your child and this may have become the basis for conversations around their hopes (and possibly fears) or interest in the donor. If you have information about your donor that you have not yet shared with your child then you might want to think about starting to do that…or at least offering it, not least because of the opportunity for conversations to open up. You may find that your child has no interest whatsoever or at least is not prepared to talk about their curiosity just at the moment or you may find they are harbouring expectations of finding someone who looks like them, shares their interests and could play a part in their life. Just having a chat about their hopes and fears in the years leading up to 18 can help manage their expectations and put a framework of potential realities around finding the donor and contact with him or her.

> Your role as a parent is first of all to manage your own feelings and then to help your children express theirs through intermittent but consistent chats throughout the teenage years. Not 'sit-down' moments but with you taking the initiative, if they don't, whilst sharing a walk, a meal or just doing something together. Try starting a conversation with, "I've been thinking about when you turn 18 and can ask about your donor. Just wondering how you feel about it."

Addressing your own feelings may be more challenging than listening to those of your child but thoughts and fears shared often means problems halved and strategies decided on. Talking with other people, a friend, someone from DC Network or one of the experienced counsellors sourced via the HFEA can be a real help. My husband's and my worst fear for our daughter, who has a strong interest in finding her donor but as a 1985 conceived person has no rights to do so, is that the donor would either reject her or not be a very nice person. We have no worries about her rejecting us – our relationship is too strong for that – but we are concerned for her. Your biggest fear may be the introduction into the family of someone who feels like a stranger but who has an irrefutable genetic link to your child. They may have an uncanny physical resemblance to them and share talents and traits or appear to be nothing like them at all. Genes work in strange ways and different people attach very different meanings to genetic or 'blood' connections. As our daughter once said, "Genes mean everything and nothing all at the same time." As a fellow parent, who has lived with two, now adult, donor conceived children as well as one from a previous marriage conceived without help, I invite you to celebrate the differences and the samenesses, just as you have celebrated your child's development into a unique human being.

Meeting the donor

Children and young people flourish when they are loved and surrounded by people who care about their development and prospects and if one of those people is the donor, then maybe that's a bonus. In her book (see Resources section) on raising her donor conceived son Ryan, Wendy Kramer speaks of the special pleasure of watching him develop a relationship with his donor

Lance and Lance's parents who welcomed Ryan as the grandchild they thought they would never have. This example may seem exceptional, but there are accounts on Facebook groups and blogs on the internet of equally happy set ups where raising parents are loved and valued alongside new relationships with biological kin that do not have the emotional back-story of child and parent but are based on a mutual interest in exploring genetic roots.

Of course not all donor and offspring contact and/or meetings go well. Sometimes they start well and just peter out because of lack of enough interests in common. Sometimes it works, sometimes it doesn't, as in all new relationships. But if your child has expectations of something special and it doesn't turn out that way then they will need your loving and tender care, without recriminations, to recover. Managing their expectations in a balanced way is one of the most loving acts you can perform for your child in the build-up to asking for identifying information.

The future belongs to your child

You may feel you should have a say about what the future holds; after all, it may change quite radically your own definition of what constitutes your family. The reality is that these decisions will lie with your child. You are successfully supporting and guiding them in the long process of becoming independent adults, and, although the consequences might affect the whole family, the decisions about what they need to complete their own sense of identity will be theirs alone. Parents' continuing task, as ever, is to offer a non-judgemental and supportive ear to whatever they wish to share with you. You might remember while your child was younger the advice was always to be prepared for the next stage of their development, including their developing understanding of donor conception and its meaning. It's the same now. You won't know whether or when your child might decide it's important to them to seek out the donor, but you can be prepared to acknowledge your own mixed feelings to yourself (and to each other, if you are part of a couple). The sudden jump from a long-settled view of your child's donor kin as unknown shadowy entities to real individuals with names and their own lives might be challenging, and need time to adjust to.

Half-siblings

Brothers and sisters you have been raised with can be a wonderful blessing and also a real pain in the neck – often at the same time. But, as with everything, feelings can change over the years. I don't recall particularly liking or loving my younger brother and sister when we were growing up, but as adults all three of us are good friends and hugely valued supporters of each other. We are lucky, it doesn't always work out that way.

Siblings raised together are always rivals for parental attention. They form bonds through living together and shared childhood history but rivalry nearly always touches part of the relationship and can lead to resentments building up over the years. All of which makes half siblings not raised together an interesting prospect.

The donor conceived young people I interviewed for this booklet nearly all showed real curiosity about half-siblings, even if they were uninterested in their donor. Whilst the donor often feels like a remote figure who would be someone from another generation, half-sibs, who will mostly be of a roughly similar age, feel like people you could have something in common with and might like to get to know.

I talked to one pair of boy/girl half-sibs who were nearly 18 at the time of interview. Ruby's mum and dad needed to use a sperm donor to conceive her and her brother who is four years younger. Raphy is an only child being brought up in two lesbian households. His genetic mother and her partner split up when Raphy was nearly five and both women have new partners. Raphy spends his time equally between his two mums. Ruby and Raphy's parents met at a DC Network meeting when the children were about three. They all got on together and lived in the same area, so met for playdates with the children. After a while one of the parents noticed that Ruby and Raphy were showing similarities in looks and mannerisms. The mothers compared notes and discovered that not only had they attended the same clinic but they had a donor with the same number (UK clinics used to give donor numbers to parents who asked for them). As the families continued to meet and spend holidays together Ruby and Raphy developed a friendship that has continued to this day. They have never gone to the same school so have valued having a 'home friend' and being opposite sex have never felt in direct competition with each other. It has occasionally been difficult explaining who the other is to outside friends, but these days most people know and just take the relationship as half-sibs for granted. Ruby's brother is of course another half-sib to Raphy and the two enjoy football talk together, but Raphy's main friendship is with Ruby who shares life stages with him. All three are sporty, not something any of the genetic parents lay a claim to!

Helen, now 22 and just finishing at university, was raised as the only child of her solo mum. As an eleven or twelve year old she became very interested in contact with half-siblings. Her mum posted information about the donor she had used on a donor linking part of DC Network's old forum and a lesbian family, actually looking for contact with another DC child about to move to secondary school, stumbled on the information and realised that their daughter was conceived with the same donor. They were shocked at the realisation as they hadn't been looking for half-sibs. After tentative and anonymous approaches to Helen's mum they slowly realised that introducing the girls would not be a threat to their family. Another girl sibling, also being raised in a same sex family, was identified at a DC Network conference only about a year later. The girls were all around 12 at the time and have been good friends ever since. They saw a lot of each other when they were younger and used to go on holiday together but are now at different universities around the country. The contact is more by messaging these days but they make sure they get together at Christmas.

Finding her two sisters (as the young women refer to each other) has been very important for Helen. When I asked her what is was she valued in her relationship with them, she said, "We know we are related, so that makes a difference. There is an unspoken assumption and level of trust that is different to a normal friend. We looked for similarities when we were younger but not so much now. I cannot imagine not being in contact with them. Genetics feel meaningful to me."

Raphy and Ruby also seem to have this unspoken trust between them. When I asked them if they would want to keep up contact if they didn't actually get on together, they were floored at first but then said that the genetic tie was meaningful to them and that they would maintain contact, but probably much more loosely, if they didn't get on. Raphy used the word 'certainty' about the relationship, meaning that it would always be there, unlike a friendship that did not have a genetic component.

Could it be that it is easier for half-siblings, not raised together, to have an amicable relationship as they are not having to compete for parental attention and can choose to spend time together rather than being forced into close proximity by growing up in the same family?

Helen, her sisters and Raphy are all only children. Ruby has a full sibling but he is quite a bit younger than her. It could be that finding a half-sib feels more important to only children, but it also appears that half-sib relationships may have a different quality about them. I have certainly heard donor conceived teenagers in families where there are two or more children, say that their interest in half-sibs is not so keen because they feel they already have siblings (even if they do have to compete with them) but it may be that if a half-sib turned up they would discover a different (not necessarily better or worse) relationship. For example, our own adult daughter would love to find a half-sib sister but is less interested in males because she has two brothers (actually also genetic half-sibs because one was conceived with a different sperm donor and one was conceived without help in my first marriage, but she was raised with them).

I have come across one instance in my interviews where siblings conceived from the same donor and raised together have different views about searching and I have read of several more on Facebook groups. Although full siblings often really value having the same donor, differences in feelings about making contact with genetic relatives has the potential for conflict. The two brothers I interviewed are both aware of how the other feels and I suspect one will not make a move without consent from his brother. Both are very protective of their much loved non-genetically connected father. Having different donors can allow more freedom of action. In our own family, Zannah's interest in finding half-sibs and/or her donor does not impinge on her brothers' disinterest in the subject. But as an adult Zannah has said that she wishes she and her brother shared a donor, so you can't win!

Lucy, 15, from a lesbian couple family, said it is very important to her that she and her brothers and sister share a sperm donor. She feels it gives them something in common in a family that is 'different' in several ways.

Of the DC adults who post in mixed Facebook groups, those who have found half-siblings seem delighted to have done so. There are a small number of instances where they feel they have little in common but most feel that finding a half-sib has added to their sum of knowledge about themselves and given richness to their lives.

As I said at the beginning of this section, most of the DC young people I interviewed had a curiosity about half-siblings, even if they had not yet acted on it. There was far less ambivalence about half-siblings than about donors.

How do you as a parent feel?

If yours is an only child you might feel that finding one or more half-sibs would be beneficial for your child as someone to share their thoughts and feelings with. Solo mums with one child often feel this way and deliberately seek half-sibs, often before their child turns 18. Certainly both Helen and her sisters and Raphy and Ruby are very positive about connections from a young age. But they all came to know their half-sibs through DC Network meetings and not via searching on social media or DNA testing, which are the most common ways that siblings are connecting these days.

You may recall from Helen's story that the parents of her first half-sib were shocked when it became obvious that they shared a donor with Helen's mum. They were concerned about the integrity of their family if another child made a familial connection with their daughter. Maybe you feel this way too. If you do you won't be the first person. On the face of it, it is very peculiar to think about children who are genetically related to your own child being raised in an unknown family, possibly of a different type/style/culture to your own and potentially having values that do not align with yours. Your child's feelings about connecting to half-siblings may be very different to yours. Some young donor-conceived people feel they cannot see some of their talents, interests and personality traits reflected in the family they grow up in. They may be hoping to find these in common with a half-sibling. This sometimes leads to high and maybe unrealistic expectations. Just as in forming friendships, there are elements of risk, particularly if both sides want different things from the relationship. Your child might find they need your sympathetic ear in trying to untangle the importance (or not) of a genetic connection to half-sibs. If you find yourself feeling a bit defensive about your child not finding all they need in your family, it might help to think about your own family and those you know. No family can possibly provide the perfect comprehensive upbringing.

Ruby's mum told me that she and her partner felt very comfortable sharing donor number information with Raphy's parents, but she attributed this to the fact of them all having become friends before the coincidence was discovered. She didn't know them well but felt that there was a connection and level of trust that helped them feel safe about the information being known. She contrasted the trust she felt with Raphy's parents with the shock of being asked to share her donor number with a woman in the waiting room at her clinic.

Parents sometimes worry about the number of half-siblings there might be growing up in other families. If your child was conceived in the UK then you can get this information from the HFEA but if you conceived abroad or with a known donor you met via an agency or on the internet, then the number of half sibs is likely to be unknown. This can feel odd, even disturbing for some parents and young people. Even under HFEA rules there could be up to twenty donor siblings through sperm donation, although this number is highly unlikely with egg or embryo donation. The oddness might be related to the fact that it is not a usual family experience (and as parents we've all tried so hard to create our normal family!). You, or your child, might be feeling a loss of specialness, of being unique. You might feel that one or two new half-siblings might be welcome, but suppose twenty emerge? There are potential links to a whole range of new relatives, whose values and lifestyles might be very different from yours; there may be expectations of contact and communication that you feel your family hasn't signed up for. The way forward might be to try to remain open to the possibilities of these new relationships but remember that if your child is under 18 you retain control over what you feel is right for your family. After that time the young adult(s) are in charge, but if relationships are close they are hopefully consulting you too. It is helpful to remember that once a genetic link is made it cannot be unmade…but of course many of us have genetic relatives we have very weak links with, sometimes not even on a Christmas card basis.

If finding half-sibs feels important to your older teenager/young adult, unlike Helen's half-sibs where parents made the first moves, your children are likely to be taking the steps towards finding them for themselves. Although they are now fully or semi-independent they are likely to hugely value your support so that their excitement and/or disappointment can be shared in the family. Evidence is increasingly showing that if parents are unsupportive or hostile then this will not prevent a young person from searching – they will simply do it secretly and not share their findings or their feelings with you. The parents of Helen's first half-sib decided to take the risk. They proceeded slowly but were reassured by Helen's mum's response. All three families now know how valuable the relationship between the three young women is. The parents are not related, as they would be if the girls were cousins, and do not necessarily socialise themselves, but they all recognise the importance of the girls to each other.

Terminology

You may have been surprised that Helen refers to her half-sibs as sisters. This is what they feel like to her: all female, close in age and similar in values and interests. Ruby and Raphy call each other half-sibs. Maybe this is because they are different genders and have different interests, but they are at the same life stage and share enough to find it important to keep in contact with each other. Maybe it is because Ruby already has a brother. What feels important is that the relationships between the three girls and the boy/girl pair are embedded in the emotional life of their families. All the parents involved are completely accepting and supportive of these relationships, which as a result feel very normal to all parties.

Half-siblings seem to have a special place in the lives of many of those who have found each other. You might like to have a chat with your child about how they would like their half-sibling to be referred to, and be ready with some suggestions if they are stuck. Some children might prefer to use a term like 'best friend' or 'special friend', which emphasises the social aspect and minimises the genetic one. Others may feel that best friends can and do change, and choose a term that makes it clear there is a permanent relatedness, like 'cousin'. It doesn't really matter that this term isn't technically correct, if your child is comfortable with it. A criteria might be that their chosen term is unlikely to provoke questions or require further explanation.

Thinking about Genes and DNA Testing

Genes

You will have noticed that a recurring theme in this booklet has been around the meanings that are placed on genes and genetic connections. A whole section in the Chapter on Preparing Your Child for the Future was devoted to Re-visiting Feelings about Genes and the two sets of half-siblings I interviewed both felt that the genetic link gave them a special feeling of trust and connection. But the meanings placed upon genes and how they contribute to someone's sense of identity exist dynamically within the cultures and society in which we live and have certainly changed over time.

In the last decades of the previous century, nurture tended to dominate over nature in the way both experts and the public thought about the way individuals come to be the people they are. Partly as a result of the completion of the human genome project in 2003 when it became possible to read nature's complete genetic blueprint for a human being, the pendulum has swung towards nature. However, most geneticists and psychologists are keen to acknowledge that environment plays a huge part in the potential modification of how genes are expressed.

Despite the caution of many experts, we are bombarded in the media with assumptions that genetics are largely responsible for determining our health and our behaviour. The long-running 'Who Do You Think You Are' and 'Long Lost Family' TV programmes suggest strongly that genes are of great interest and importance. They imply that genealogy is more than just a niche hobby; filling in 'missing links' can play a huge part in helping to complete our identity. Yet, like thousands of families, your experience is that it is the everyday care and love that makes you parents and shapes your child, not genetic bonds. This ambiguity might feel confusing, but equally, it might help to separate out your irreplaceable role as your child's parent from their task of finding what best helps them to complete a sense of their own identity. If your child decides to embark on a search for unknown genetic relatives, they are not being 'disloyal' to you or your family. They are adding to the values and experiences you have given them, rather than deciding to replace them.

Genes and genetic connections are undeniably important but they are not the only way in which valued relationships and a lasting kinship are formed.

As Nordquist and Smart found in their exceptional book Relative Strangers: Family Life, Genes and Donor Conception, genes can mean a huge amount and absolutely nothing, all at the same time; the same conclusion our daughter came to. Parents and grandparents can talk in the same breath about loving a child to bits whilst having quite complicated feelings about genetic inheritance. Mixed feelings are in essence part of donor conception family life and if you have them about DNA testing you are not alone.

DNA Testing

It is only since about 2016 that it has become clear that anonymity can no longer be promised for current and future donors of all egg, sperm and embryos and that formerly anonymous donors cannot count on not being found. Direct-to-consumer DNA testing has exploded into society in general and expanded at an exponential rate. It has revolutionised the donor conception world. Debbie Kennett, a genealogical researcher wrote in early 2018, *"We are entering uncharted territory now that donor anonymity can be so easily circumvented. The combination of DNA testing, online databases and large social networking websites means that it can be easy to track down and contact newly found genetic relatives. What is the etiquette for contacting your newly identified donor who was promised anonymity? What are the obligations of the donor to respond to contact? How will these discoveries affect other family members?"*

You may be surprised to learn that a donor does not have to be in any of the databases to be found, as identification can be made from matches with cousins combined with traditional genealogical research or making connections through platforms like Facebook or LinkedIn. Debbie Kennett goes on to explain –

"It all depends on the number of close matches and how much detail they've provided about their family tree. With a few close matches it would be possible to identify likely candidates and it may be that there is only one candidate who is in the right place at the right time. With the growing databases identification could in theory also be possible with a network of more distant cousins…as more and more people test, people will increasingly get matched with second cousins or closer when they first test."

The biggest DNA companies in the UK are 23andme.com, familytreedna.com and ancestry.co.uk followed by myheritage.com and livingdna.com. They vary a little in what they offer: 23andme and Ancestry offer both genealogy and information on how your DNA relates to certain health conditions and inherited risk factors. The highest take-up for these companies is in the USA, UK, Australia, New Zealand, Scandinavia and Ireland, but they are expanding into new areas all the time. Their websites emphasise how simple the process is and how much fun it will be *('Trace your family story with a family tree – we make it easy'; 'Your DNA test offers you the powerful experience of discovering what makes you unique and learning where you really come from'.)* They don't, however, offer any support following surprising findings, other than standard customer services.

You might think from media stories and also Debbie Kennett's words above that DNA testing inevitably turns up donors, half-siblings, cousins, aunts and uncles. In fact for most people a third cousin is the closest match they are liable to get. Our daughter knows this only too well. She and I have tested with 23andMe and AncestryDNA and no close relatives have come to light. If she wished to spend a long time tracing family trees, searching old records and triangulating people's names, something might come up, but so far she has not chosen to go down that road. The difficulty for some people might be living with initial disappointment and also knowing that new close relatives might pop up at any time. The task is how to find a place to put it so that it doesn't disrupt the rest of your life – both for the DC young adult and for parents. For some, I imagine, feelings might unexpectedly change from initial take-it-or-leave-it curiosity to a real sense of incompleteness and disappointment.

Kate, 26, has always felt comfortable being donor conceived and has spoken at DCN and other events about her thoughts and feelings about it many times. Her interest in her donor has always been pretty low but as an only child her curiosity about half-siblings had gone up and down over the years. Finally, in her mid twenties, she decided to take a DNA test with the express purpose of identifying half siblings if possible. What she wasn't expecting was to find an uncle! She contacted him and after a couple of months he came back saying that both he and his brother had donated sperm but his brother was the only one to help create children. He gave Kate his brother's email address (with his permission). She told her parents and eventually, after long gap, emailed the donor who had viewed her LinkedIn profile which she found very weird. It took Kate ages to craft her email but he responded and said he would be happy to tell her about his background and family. He also changed his status with the HFEA to become identifiable and signed up to 23andme.

Throughout this saga Kate has kept her parents in the loop as she didn't want anything to be a secret. It turned out that they were more curious than her but also concerned for her. When I spoke to Kate in late 2019, she said she probably owed her donor an email as it had been a couple of months since his last one. She is taking things slowly but has been surprised to find how much contact with this man has meant to her. The story continues.

If your teenager or young adult child mentions to you about possibly doing a DNA test, talk with them about what it is they are hoping to find and try and discover, in as unobtrusive way as possible, how much they know about what is and isn't possible to find and what their hopes and expectations are. It's best to support your child in finding out as much as they can themselves, although you might have done some research yourself. Do bear in mind that what they probably won't discover easily is that it can be helpful for the genetic parent to also give a DNA sample to the same company so that his or her DNA can be ruled out and the information given becomes more accurate. It is also helpful to know before going ahead that some of the different functions within the DNA testing platform can be switched on or off. For instance, by answering questions offered at the beginning it is possible just to discover the (rough) geographical origins of ancestors without being shown (the much more accurate) DNA relatives. Sometimes this is all DC people are interested in, at least to start with anyway. They also need to know that they might find someone they are not looking for, as in Kate's story.

A tube of spit sent to a distant address in a cardboard package can lead to the knowledge your child wishes to have, show up nothing of particular interest or it may turn up information they really were not prepared for.

The book Finding Our Families: A First-of-its-Kind Book for Donor Conceived People and their Families by Wendy Kramer and Naomi Cahn can be useful reading for both parents and children. The first section deals with 'telling', something you will have successfully managed earlier, but the second half is a guide to searching for genetically linked relatives, including the complex etiquette of approaching someone you have discovered via a DNA test, like a half-sibling, who may or may not know they are donor conceived or that a parent has been a donor.

By showing an interest but not panicking or trying to take over, your teenager is far more likely to involve you in the project and this will open opportunities to talk about their expectations, hopes and fears, as discussed earlier. You are likely to have your own mixed feelings about what a DNA test might reveal but best to keep these to yourself (and your partner if you are in a couple) and focus on supporting your child.

There was a lot of ambivalence around DNA testing, particularly for donor information, in the group of DC young people I interviewed. Seventeen-year-old egg donor conceived Isabella said that she was interested but only in geographical heritage rather than genetic relatives for the time being. Adam, also 17, didn't really want to discuss it and said he had come to terms with never being able to know. Harriet, who is 23, has curiosity about her appearance but has never considered taking a DNA test. She wonders what purpose connection to the donor or half sibs would serve and doesn't feel that other DC people are "her tribe". Her (full) brother Ben, 26, found his curiosity about genetic relatives aroused by talking to me but said that it hadn't really occurred to him before. Ellie, 19, didn't know anything about DNA testing but when I mentioned it said she would be worried about rejection by the donor. However, some of the older group had moved on from earlier mixed feelings and decided to test. Kate, whose story appears above, is one of them, our daughter another and Sam, 28, whom I spoke to twice. On the first occasion he had pretty equivocal feelings about testing but apparently his conversation with me stirred up interest and by the time a Christmas Eve ad on his phone for a sale of DNA kits appeared, he was ready to buy one. As he was very busy he didn't actually do the test until late February 2020 and results six weeks later showed only a multitude of third to fifth cousins. As he explained to me in our second chat, his interest in the whole thing is at a pretty low level and he doesn't intend to pursue it further.

Rachel, an American DC adult who was raised in a solo mum but also extended multi-generational family, took a DNA test some years ago when she was in her mid-twenties. It took three years for her to find her first half-sibling and after five years she found the donor, whom she refers to as dad. She has now found several half-siblings and they keep popping up. These connections are incredibly important to her and as she said in her email to me, "talking to another donor conceived person feels like I am talking to one of my tribe."

Jessica, 27, from the States and brought up in a heterosexual couple family, told me, "I have been curious about my biological father and half-siblings for my entire life. I have spent hundreds of dollars on DNA testing websites and have called the clinic looking for information. For years, I felt sad that I never found any biological family. However, several months ago, I found a half-sister on one of the websites. I started crying with joy when I saw her face and how much we looked alike. However, she did not know she was donor conceived, so she had to deal with the knowledge that her parents lied to her over and over throughout her life. This has created a barrier for me in developing a closer relationship with my sister."

These are just some of the enormously wide range of feelings about genetic connections and DNA testing that exist amongst donor conceived young adults. It is impossible to know how your child or children will feel as they move through adolescence and into adulthood and indeed whether or not those feelings will change over time. All we as parents can do is keep in touch, stay interested and be ready to offer an encouraging nod, a listening ear, or a supportive hand to hold.

Solo Mum and Same Sex Families

Most of the issues addressed in this booklet affect all types of family. Everyone, no matter their family, goes through puberty and adolescence, emerging into young adulthood at 18. All early-told donor conceived children and teenagers have to incorporate the knowledge of their 'different' beginnings into their identity as they grow and develop.

The welcome combination of medical advances and changes in societal views now allows families to be created in many ways, and this means a significant and growing number of young people will belong in solo mum, lesbian or gay families. However, it remains true that heterosexual families are seen as the norm and the 'gold standard'. As such, other family types regularly find themselves measured against them, even though of course 'mum and dad' families are no guarantee of providing a stable and loving upbringing. If yours is a solo mum, lesbian or gay family, you are very likely to have attracted personal questions which no heterosexual family would have to face. The questioners may not mean to be intrusive, but rather curious, interested and well-meaning; but the effect can be that you - and your child – feel that you have to explain yourselves.

Young people's thoughts and feelings

I interviewed six young people from solo mum families (two of whose mothers were also lesbian) and two teenagers from lesbian couple families. No teenagers from gay dad or trans families came forward to be interviewed. A group of just eight is not a scientific sample but it is interesting to note that all of the young people mentioned that their family type had been much more challenging for them to manage over the years than the fact that they were donor conceived. You might find some of the views expressed here surprising and maybe difficult to hear. But we need to recognise the honesty of those giving their thoughts, without which we cannot acknowledge their reality.

The young people I spoke to described a range of both positive and negative feelings about their family situations. By the time I spoke to them, most felt that they were accepted by their friends for who they were and did not have to explain either their family type or beginnings any longer. One or two of my interviewees felt their situation worked in their favour: Lucy, the youngest at 15, found that she gained social status at her girls school both by being part of a lesbian family and because she is donor conceived.

During conversations with the eight young people the whole issue of Dads brought up a range of feelings about the impact of not having a dad, both throughout their lives to this point and now. For Billy, who comes from a solo mum family, entrance into traditional male society in terms of things like going to the pub and supporting a football team had felt difficult and he wondered if he would have been less sensitive and tougher if he'd had a dad. He was, however, at 20, beginning to find his tribe in the climbing and running communities. Billy also felt that having two parents was probably a better set up. He said it was hard to argue with his mum and not have another parent to go to (citing good cop, bad cop). He has been 'teetering on the edge' of taking steps to find out about his donor for a while.

Not all the young men I spoke to felt like Billy but sport definitely featured in their wish list. Adam said that a dad might have got him into football earlier but added that he had a lot of father figures around him (particularly via his synagogue) so it wasn't really a problem. Raphy definitely wished that his mums, or at least one of them, was sporty and he sometimes felt wistful when seeing male friends go off to watch sport with their dads. From a parents' perspective, Caroline pointed out that "everyone's interests are different whatever family type they are, but it can be difficult for a solo mum to attend events with loads of dads with their sons there."

As has been emphasised in earlier chapters, how children perceive and deal with their family type and their DC origins varies hugely. Some of the young people I spoke to have been grappling with difficult and critical perceptions of their parents' choices.

As a young teenager Demi, 22, was embarrassed by being DC, only told close friends and swore them to secrecy. She longed to have a second parent and siblings, 'a normal family unit'. Although she admits that all decisions to have a child are probably selfish, she thinks her mother's choice was a selfish one, although she likes knowing she was wanted. As she reached middle adolescence she found being DC was almost a 'cool' thing to be but found many people's questions to be intrusive.

Ellie, 19, whose solo mum is also lesbian, would rather have had two parents, even if they had been separated. She says she was a bit resentful in her early teen years around little things like there only being two of them to carry out household tasks and no-one to give her lifts anywhere. Other people (with divorced or separated parents) say they are in the same position as her, but she knows they are not.

Rachel, now in her mid-thirties and an only child of a solo mum, was the only DC adult I interviewed who has really felt hurt and angry that her (donor) dad did not choose to raise her, although I have come across quite a few others on Facebook groups. "Who allows some stranger to raise his or her yet to be conceived biological child without vetting the person first?" She also said, "As I've gotten older, I realised that my mom's want or desire for a baby was really about her and not about me. Accordingly, being wanted by my mum doesn't give me the warm fuzzies like it used to do when I was very little."

However, others I spoke to had arrived at different views:
Helen, 23, daughter of a solo mum, first noticed that her family was different when she was six or seven but finding her half-sisters when she was 12 has helped and, as she said, "As I have got older more and more families seem to be different in some way anyway."

Lucy, 15, was the only interviewee of the eight who did not mention not having a dad. Perhaps it is because she has two parents living together (both female), a sister and two brothers. All the children are from the same sperm donor. Lucy was conceived by one of her mums and the other three (including twins) are from her other mum.

As mentioned above, family type rather than being donor conceived seemed to be particularly problematic during the early teens. The pressures to 'fit in' in early secondary school years can be immense and being seen to be 'different' in almost any way can feel dangerous. Ellie, who had been bullied in primary school (although not about having a lesbian mum or being DC), made sure she kept as neutral and under the radar as possible for most of her secondary school life. Others certainly found themselves the object of curiosity and questioning at times but found that confidence and a certain bravado mostly saw them through. These are not issues that are faced by children from heterosexual couple families where donor conception can be concealed by being part of a mum and dad family, if children choose to keep it that way.

How do you feel?

It is worth reiterating here that most of the young people in this group felt at the time of interview that they were doing well and no longer felt pressured to explain themselves, their family or beginnings. You will have noticed a wide variation of views and feelings; one young person believed her family and donation type conferred positive social status, whilst another was angry with the whole practice of anonymous gamete donation. It is important to remember this because some of the comments from the young people make for potentially uncomfortable reading. It may well be particularly hard to hear that your child is not necessarily as proud of their family as you, their parent, would hope.

I invite you to look at these views as an opportunity for you to think about how you would like to react if your child has some of these feelings. Firstly, it's important to start by thinking about what emotions and feelings these comments bring up for you. It is possible they might reawaken fears and insecurities you experienced when making your decision to start a family. They might challenge your hope that the lack of a male figure, or a second parent can't matter too much because, after all, creating a loving and nurturing environment gives a child everything they need for security and growth… doesn't it? They might just make you feel sad, and bring up memories of times when you felt inadequate despite your best efforts. It's important to acknowledge these feelings because otherwise it's difficult to really hear the pain, sadness or anger that might lie behind the young person's comments. It is also true that it might be a relief to be able to talk to your child about a difficult situation that you witnessed them going through from a more adult perspective. As with all parents and all parenting, your ability to see situations and experiences through their eyes as well as your own adult ones brings the balance and wisdom that is required in the face of difficult feelings.

You might be thinking that teenagers and young people go through phases, and you could be right. It's a lengthy process of making sense of their place in the world. Try thinking back to your own teenage years and you will probably remember feeling some strong criticisms of pretty much every aspect of how your parents lived their lives, which you may or may not have voiced. If your parent had told you it was just a stage you were going through might you have felt dismissed and unheard? You may recall in Chapter Two on Developmental Stages we explored the task for adolescents of finding their own identity, and one common way of doing this is to separate their views and values from those of their parent(s). This may well include the decisions and values you have attached to donor conception. It may be that some of the feelings voiced by these young people are transitory, but equally some may consolidate and form part of your adult child's sense of themselves. It makes no difference to the real strength of feeling of the young person voicing those thoughts here and now. You may not want to hear it, but it is far better for a child to be able to share these feelings than to sense that they need to hide them from you. In discussing how to talk with your child about their donor conception origins, we often stress how vital it is to accept whatever feelings your child has, and this is no different, though it may be much harder for you.

Billy's mum Martha talked about her son being very emotionally literate. She also described how he has struggled with learning because of dyslexia and mild dyspraxia, but through his determination he has achieved good A levels and is due to start university soon. She said that Billy had at times expressed a wish for a dad and shown curiosity about his donor and that she would be totally supportive if he decides to go ahead with a search for his donor. Martha said being a solo mum obviously has its challenges but that the donor conception angle has never been a problem. She is not in touch with other solo mums but said friends had been a vital support in Billy's growing up.

Ellie's mum Sarah told me that she had been in a lesbian relationship when Ellie was conceived but that her partner had left after a year. She had not intended to be a solo mum. She was only too aware of Ellie's reluctance to draw attention to herself as being DC following being bullied at primary school. Sarah hopes that she has made time to listen to Ellie's difficult feelings and her advice to other parents is, if your child/teenager needs to talk about something, stop what you are doing (no matter how inconvenient it is) and listen. She also advises not taking things too personally and not over-responding.

If your child feels it's safe enough to communicate at least some less positive feelings to you, and senses you are able to accept and acknowledge them, it can lead on to supportive discussions about coping strategies for action they may want to take. Think back to your own coping strategies at times when you have felt life to be more difficult as a lesbian or single woman. Your lived experience is invaluable, and will be the main positive influence for your child. You will also know what fits with your own child's personality and with their social environment.

Lucia has 13 year old boy/girl twins conceived in Spain using a donor embryo. Her daughter has recently voiced more strongly than ever her opinions and feelings about Lucia's choices regarding her conception. She is frustrated that her choice to meet and know her donors was removed from the start by Lucia's choice of anonymous donors.

Lucia told me that her daughter had recently taken a commercial DNA test which has revealed some ethnicity information she is very pleased about. However, her daughter expresses resentment that it has to be up to her a donor conceived child, to pursue this way of finding her genetic family. Lucia said, "I find this very hard to hear but I feel I must hear it and continue to listen to her. I owe this to my daughter as my choices have directly affected her feelings."

The range of the young people's comments illustrates that you cannot second guess the opinion your child will come to as a young person or adult about their donor conception origins. Everyone has their own unique personality, temperament and individual experience, and this will shape the feelings that they have about all aspects of their life, including being donor conceived. Some young people will find it easy to have a sense of perspective on how their family and circumstances fit in with the general shape of today's society. Others may come to a view that donor conception is not a simple alternative to a more traditional family. It might be hard to read these less positive views, but it can help you think again about what might be going on for a young person who is struggling with difficult feelings. Some of the young people quoted here have a strong sense of unfairness; the feeling that their peers don't have the same issues to contend with. Your own experiences of dealing with this through your own life could be really useful here. In addition, you may find that the bullet points listed under More Things That Can Help in the next chapter are of use.

Another fundamental question raised by a couple of young people is whether the desire to be a parent is always selfish – one of the questions which solo or lesbian mothers themselves often have before deciding to have a family. For lesbian and solo mums it will almost certainly be true that you gave even more thought than heterosexual parents to your decision. You will have considered the practical implications and the potential cost of being seen to be different by wider society. You will have concluded that you had the resources to do this well. At the same time you, like all who are considering donor conception, will have been driven by a strong desire to go to some lengths to create a family, to offer your child unconditional love and nurture. So yes, this part is 'selfish'; but no more so than anybody's decision to create a family, whether by donor conception or not.

Adam's mum Debra has always been a very independent person and says Adam is like her in this. They are part of a Jewish community that has been very supportive to them and provided father figures for Adam. Debra told me that being a solo mum has been much more difficult, particularly financially, than anything to do with donor conception. Her aunt has been very important in their lives and sometimes provided money for Adam to be able to do things, although he started working at 15, alongside his schooling. Both mother and son were very positive about their lives.

Advice from DC Young People and... Last Words

I hope this booklet has given you food for thought not only about your children's needs as they grow and change but also about your needs as a parent. How do YOU feel now about the decisions you made so many years ago and what sort of shape do you think you are in for going into a future that might or might not include your children's half-siblings and/or genetic parent(s)? I can imagine that your feelings might be very mixed. If you feel there are areas that still need exploring then it is never too late to seek some supportive counselling (which DC Network may be able to help guide you to). If you are simply unclear, and maybe excited and/or unsure about what the future may hold, then hang in there. Mixed or ambivalent feelings are normal and can actually be helpful; they allow you to adjust more easily to whatever it is that does happen, rather than assuming all will be well or all will be terrible, which are fixed positions that may be difficult to move on from.

Mixed or ambivalent feelings are normal for our children too. As parents we want our children to be happy and this can lead to trying to 'rescue' them from difficult feelings or 'fix' them in some way. As American psychotherapist Jana Rupnow says, "By insisting that a child 'look on the bright side' or focus on all the great things in their lives, you could come across as dismissive. By minimising negative feelings you could inadvertently give the message that your child is not allowed to feel anything but positive about his or her donor conception. We all have a mixture of positive, negative and neutral feelings about life. Ambivalent feelings are more realistic; there are usually two sides to a story. By allowing your child to feel and express all their feelings with you, you create a safe space between you and encourage moments of bonding." As Jane and I know, these moments become rarer and more precious as they move into teenage and young adult years.

Again Rupnow says, "Each family has to agree to levels of communication about the topic, but your teens will soon be adults making independent decisions. The teenage years require you to make a shift in how you parent." If you are baffled and confused at times then consider this a normal state as a parent of a teenager. If communication feels difficult (or you'd like to be more prepared for this), I join Jana Rupnow in recommending the book How to Talk So Teens Will Listen and Listen So Teens Will Talk by Adele Faber and Elaine Mazlish as pure gold. Briefly, say less and listen more. Guide them in finding their own solutions by asking pertinent questions. Avoid dismissing or diminishing their feelings.

More Things That Can Help:

- Try not to take things too personally
- Try not to over-respond or become defensive
- Remember teenagers and young adults often have very different views on many things (not just their conception or family type) and feelings can run high
- Sometimes simply feeling that you have been heard is what's most important for your child
- Think about your own support networks and identify friends who you may be able to talk to as a parent
- Talk to other DC parents, particularly those who have been through similar experiences
- Consider speaking with a specialist counsellor who has knowledge in this area.

What I learned from interviewing young DC people

All but two of the 21 young people I interviewed were either DCN members in their own right or the offspring of long-standing DCN members. Some came forward following the appeal via the DCN Bulletin and Facebook groups and some were approached by me. They were all told of their DC beginnings from a very young age. As you will have seen from the quotes throughout the booklet, they had a very wide range of feelings about their lives as donor conceived people. The good news is that the vast majority felt comfortable with who they are and the state of their lives, in relation to their donor conception, at the time of interview, but most recognised that their thoughts and feelings might change in the future. Two young women from heterosexual couple families felt that donors' rights to continued anonymity should be respected but most thought that all DC people should have the right to access information about their donor if they felt they needed it. However, one young man thought that this access should only be with involvement of an intermediary to support the process. Some of the young people who would not have the right to identifiable information at 18 were envious of those who could, but others were not. There was no difference between the family types of young people who held these views.

I did not ask all interviewees about whether or not they told people they were in a regular relationship with about DC because it felt intrusive with those I did not know well. Also dating is something that teenagers are unlikely to discuss with their parents, but I thought these quotes from three young women were of interest. Kate, 26, whom I have known for a number of years said, "My boyfriend Will has known me since uni so has always been au fait with DC stuff - as with most of my friends/colleagues/people I meet in the pub. I was very happy to chat about it with him and so it's never been a 'Thing To Be Brought Up'. I apply the same openness and assumptions of goodwill to partners as I do to everyone, more or less." Our daughter Zannah, now settled with a partner, told me that her heritage had always come up early with boyfriends, or anyone new really, because of her height (she is 6ft) and her Scandinavian looks. She was always happy to talk about being donor conceived but like Kate, didn't feel it was something that Had To Be Brought Up. Harriet, 23, however, does think about being DC when she is dating someone new and will always make sure that she makes the information known at some point and will often joke about the man being DC himself or his dad having been a sperm donor.

Many parents worry whether social media will be used to bully and intimidate their child about their beginnings. I asked my interviewees whether this had ever happened and no-one said that it had. Very few of the young people had used the internet to look up anything to do with donor conception or to try to find genetic connections. Three or four belonged to one of the Facebook (FB) groups, either a mixed one or just for donor conceived people alone but only my two American participants said they were active members of any groups. I think Jessica, 27, from Atlanta summed up the feeling of both women when she said, "While my friends and family have been supportive, they have not experienced the complicated feelings that can occur when you are donor conceived. Therefore, my membership in Facebook groups for donor conceived people have been a great source of support. I recently met other donor conceived people in person for the first time in my life. I was elated to find people like me who understood my feelings and experiences."

I have heard very positive comments from other American DC people about the support they get from FB groups for donor conceived adults and was intrigued as to why they seemed to be less popular with the young people I spoke to. Two had sampled We Are Donor Conceived, the largest DC persons only group, but had not wanted to stay. It is possible this is something to do with the culture of the group, which is dominated by Americans, but I did not ask enough in-depth questions to get to the heart of this. A clue may be found in a comment made by Demi, 22, who said she had not made contact with any of the DC adults on the mixed FB group she is part of as they all seem to be American or Australian. She would like to have UK contacts. (See Resources section)

Advice from young people

What really animated the interviewees was the chance to give advice to parents. And what good advice it is. Apart from important repeated calls for honesty and openness in general and differences of opinion on whether parents should air their views or keep their opinions to themselves, here are the most pertinent pleas from teenagers and young adults –

- Don't assume you are going to be enough for your chi d. Put your own feelings aside. Don't think your child should be gratefu . Be natural, have free-flowing conversations. Teens are bound to go through confusion and curiosity. Supporting and allowing this will not damage the bond between you. Wanting to have more info and/or contact is not a threat to parents. Information belongs to your child. Confidentiality between parent and child important. Be prepared for an angry phase. Be actively support ve. This is different to just tolerating curiosity.

- Allow discussion, don't get defensive. Be supportive of whatever you child needs to do.

- Facilitating emotional issues is a parent's role. No pressure should be put on people who have no interest whatsoever in their beginnings by donat on It is OK to be curious and not curious. Most important – understand ng differences between privacy and secrecy and control of information a ter age 12ish – respect your child's right to privacy.

- Parents should let children know that they are willing to have conversations and that nothing is out of bounds. Parents should raise the topic from time to time, giving openings. Parents should make sure they are comforta le and well-informed before raising the topic.

- Talk about puberty, sex, relationships and emotions openly generally (weird things happen to body and mind as teenagers), start talking about half-sibs as a possibility and also slight chance of consanguinity (having an intimate relationship/creating a child with someone closely genetica ly related to you).

- Support your child in his or her search for biological family if your child chooses to search. Pay for their DNA tests, help them build family trees, be excited when they tell you about connections they have made, etc.

- Do not diminish the role or relationship of a biological parent

- Realise that how your child feels about donor conception is not necessarily about you or your relationship with your child. In other words, a child can love and have a wonderful relationship with his parent(s), but still question the ethics of donor conception or be disturbed by aspects of it, such as anonymity or being otherwise kept from having a relationship with a biological parent.

- Take ownership of how your choices have impacted your child. Admit your mistakes and apologise if necessary.

And most important of all, the advice from seventeen-year-old Adam about communication earlier on in the booklet.

"The way you discuss the topic will influence how your child feels about it. Treat them like an adult, offer options and LISTEN. Be ready for emotions. Make sure the focus is on their feelings and not on yours. Give your child a sense of freedom but keep a watching eye."

Some of this advice is sobering, but most is uplifting as it reveals the insightfulness and maturity of the young adults I interviewed. It also shows how much our children want us, their parents, to try and see donor conception from their point of view and support them as they manage, as all young people must, the changing world around them and their place in it. We are important to them, no matter how it may seem sometimes, so it is only right that we accept their choices and changes of mind and listen to any expressions of sadness and anger. It is also true that it is helpful for young adults to begin to see us, their parents, as separate people with feelings and views that do not necessarily agree with theirs but can be respected. This is, of course, how we all learn to negotiate with others generally.

As parents we won't necessarily get things right, but we owe it to our children to look after ourselves so that we can do the best we can at the time for them. Almost the very last words are from Claire, mother to Ben, 26 and Harriet, 23 who spoke to me about the importance of accepting each child as a unique person and how liberating it is not to expect your child to be a miniature version of yourself. As a parent to three adult children who tower over my husband and I, I can only agree with this wholeheartedly.

These very last words are from Eric Schwartzman, dad to two sperm donor conceived teenagers, resident of New York and long-time friend to DC Network. See the Resources section for his social media links.

"There are numerous ways to describe families. There are many factors that define who we are and where and who we come from. Most individuals can mentally distinguish between the dad that raised them and the man whose genetic material runs through them. It does not diminish or take away anything from me or how I love my kids to acknowledge and recognize at some point my child, my children, may want to know more than the gene sequence of their donor. That someday they may want to meet him. That they may want to know him. That they may want him in their lives in some form. I am still their dad. I am just not their biological father. Yes, nurture is a big deal. Just don't discount the nature. Your kids will appreciate that you understand that."

Further Reading and Resources

Parenting support

- Jana Rupnow
  Three Makes Baby: How to parent your donor conceived child
  Rupnow Associates publishing, Texas, 2018
  Available to buy from DC Network

  Mostly for potential parents and those parenting young children but with an excellent short section on teenagers.

- Wendy Kramer and Naomi Cahn, J.D.
  Finding Our Families: A first-of-its-kind book for donor conceived people and their families
  Penguin Group, New York, 2013

  First 'how to tell' and then questions and strategies for donor conceived adults and their parents around searching for and connecting with genetic relatives.

- Wendy Kramer
  Donor Family Matters: My story of raising a profoundly gifted donor conceived child, Redefining Family, and Building the Donor Sibling Registry
  Wendy Kramer and Donor Sibling Registry, Colorado, 2020

  An honest and heart-warming account of Wendy's path to parenthood by sperm donation, the challenges of raising a gifted child and how the Donor Sibling Registry came to be started and developed into a national and international resource for DC families.

- Adele Faber and Elaine Mazlish
  How to Talk So Teens Will Listen and Listen So Teens Will Talk
  Piccadilly Press, 2005

  Simply the best resource on communication between parents and teenagers

- Terri Apter
  The Myth of Maturity: What Teenagers Need from Parents to Become Adults
  Norton 2002
  Terri Apter, social psychologist and researcher, writes wisely and compassionately about why so many young people today are so quick to leave childhood behind but so slow to become adults.

Teenage Brain Development

All three of these books draw on research into brain development that has allowed us to understand how neural pathways develop and change during children and young people's developmental stages, particularly in the early teenage years.

- Nicola Morgan
  Blame My Brain: the amazing teenage years revealed
  Walker Books, London, 2005

- Daniel J Siegel MD
  Brainstorm: The Purposes and Power of the Teenage Brain
  Scribe UK 2017

- Josh Shipp
  The Grown-Ups Guide to Teenage Humans
  Harper Wave 2017

Novels for DC pre-teens and young teenagers

- Beverley Ward
  Archie Nolan: Family Detective,
  Donor Conception Network, UK, 2015

  A humorous, illustrated story book along the lines of the Diary of a Wimpy Kid books featuring Archie and his twin sister Jemima who are donor conceived.

- Annabelle Pitcher
  Silence is Goldfish
  UK, 2005

  15 year old Tess discovers by accident that she is donor conceived. Her subsequent refusal/inability to speak masks the turbulence of feelings and questions she is grappling with. A torch in the shape of a goldfish aids her quest for the truth.

Continued...

Petra Nordqvist and Leah Gilman
Curious Connections Project
Morgan Centre for the Study of Everyday Life
University of Manchester

For the leaflet giving a very accessible summary of the project's findings: Being an Egg or Sperm Donor: balancing 'being available' with 'knowing your place'? and information on resources about the project:
https://www.manchester.ac.uk/egg-and-sperm-donors

Petra Nordqvist and Carol Smart
Relative Strangers: Family Life, genes and donor conception
Palgrave MacMillan Hampshire, 2014

Beautifully written and very accessible account of research study looking at the family life of both heterosexual and lesbian couples, including interviews with grandparents.

Katherine Fine (editor)
Donor Conception for Life: Psychoanalyitic Reflections on New Ways of Conceiving the Family
Routledge London, 2015
Available to buy from DC Network

Much more accessible than the title would suggest, the chapters in this book reflect by way of research and personal experiences on the many ways in which becoming a parent by donor conception has changed over the years, what has stayed the same and what is different and also what the future may look like.

Susan Golombok
Modern Families: Parents and Children in New Family Forms
Cambridge University Press, Cambridge 2015.

Professor Golombok's teams, first at City University and then at the Centre for Family Research at the University of Cambridge, have led the way in researching DC children in different family types and are conducting the first longitudinal study of donor conceived children's wellbeing.

Rosanna Hertz and Margaret K. Nelson
Random Families: Genetic Strangers, Sperm Donor Siblings and the Creation of New Kin
Oxford University Press 2019

This fascinating American research looks at how families with young donor conceived children are connecting with each other in a variety of ways. At its heart is the question Do shared genes make you a family?

Debbie Kennett's article on DNA Testing referred to in the chapter on Thinking About Genes and DNA Testing can be found in
Bio-News https://www.bionews.org.uk/page_96385

The International Society of Genetic Genealogy have on their website some excellent articles about resources for donor conceived adults and guide to searching for genetic relatives, including what to think about before someone starts on this path. Follow these links –

https://isogg.org/wiki/Support_and_information_for_donor-conceived_people

https://isogg.org/wiki/Getting_ready_to_search

https://isogg.org/wiki/Getting_ready_for_contact

https://isogg.org/wiki/Information_for_donors:_getting_ready_for_contact_with_donor_offspring

People can also click on the category at the bottom of the page to see all the articles in the Wiki relating to donor conception:
https://isogg.org/wiki/Category:Donor_conception

Dani Shapiro
Inheritance: A memoir of Genealogy, Paternity and Love
Daunt Books, published 2019.
Available to buy from DC Network

This wonderful and beautifully written book contains the story of how Dani Shapiro discovered after taking a DNA test in her fifties, that she was donor conceived, found the donor and eventually made peace with her heritage from both genetic and non-genetic sources.

Continued...

Further research into the experiences of donor conceived adults and DC families can be found via the following links:

https://dsr-static-files.s3.us-west-2.amazonaws.com/485cc3a945adcfb7

https://www.researchgate.net/publication/280122837_Sperm_donors_describe_the_experience_of_contact_with_their_donor-conceived_offspring

Also see the website of the Victorian Assisted Reproduction Treatment Authority (VARTA) for excellent video films of donor conceived adults, parents by DC and donors all speaking about their lives and experiences.
https://www.varta.org.au/information-and-support/donor-conception

https://heyreprotech.substack.com/p/born-via-traditional-surrogacy-what for Alison Motluk's interview with surrogate-born Gee Roberts referred to in the section on Terminology.

Daniels, K.R.
The perspective of adult donor conceived persons.
In *Assistierte Reproduktion mit Hilfe Dritter. (eds)* Beier, Brugge
Thorn and Wiesemann. Springer 1/1/2020

Daniels, Ken.
Understanding and managing relationships in donor assisted families.
In *Donor Conception for Life.*
Kate Fine.(ed)
London. Routledge. 2015. 181-208

Social Media

For DC Young people

There are several private groups on the internet for donor conceived people and the list given below is just a start. Most are for over 18s. As you will have read in the booklet none of the UK based young people I interviewed were active on them, but the two American participants were. I do know that some older UK based DC people use these groups; possibly mostly those who were told late and/

or have parents who are unwilling to have conversations around DC matters. The largest of these groups by far for over 18s is:

We Are Donor Conceived
https://www.wearedonorconceived.com

For those over 18 interested in DNA testing
DNA for the Donor Conceived (DNA Detectives)
https://www.facebook.com/groups/

A small group for 13 to 18s is:
GenZ Donor Conceived People

Podcast
Ally's story: Half of Me: https://mytuner-radio.com/podcast/half-of-me-ally-donor-half-siblings-1453118743

Mixed Groups for DC People, Parents and Donors: these are all on Facebook
They are private groups that you have to ask to join and posts can only be seen by other members of the group. Your membership of the group cannot be seen by your FB friends.

The largest and most active of these groups is:
Donor Conceived People, Siblings, Parents and Donors: The posts on this group can become heated but it is very well moderated and bullying and intimidation absolutely not allowed. It is an education to take part or just be a silent visitor.

UK Donor Conceived Chat is a private mixed group that is used quite a lot for potential sibling matching but also for UK based DC adults and some parents.

Donor Conception Discussion Group (Egg/Sperm/Embryo/Donors/Children/Family) and **Building Bridges in the Donor Conceived World** are both splinter groups from the largest group.

Eric Schwartzman is moderator of a Facebook group for men with fertility issues/needing or using donor conception for family creation and parenting in a DC family.
https://www.facebook.com/groups/2259512504329244/?ref=share
Eric can also be found on Instagram at
Eric S (@Life_DI_Dad)
https://instagram.com/life_di_dad?igshid=yizvbbo15k7m

Useful Contacts

HFEA
For enquiries from parents of under 16s
and donor conceived people from age
16: https://www.hfea.gov.uk/contact-us

Donor Sibling Registry
Based in the United States has a website
https://donorsiblingregistry.com but
also a secret Facebook page that you
can access via Wendy Kramer: wendy@
donorsiblingregistry.org

Donor Conceived Register (UK)
For people conceived before 1991 by
donor conception and those who donated
before this date.
Enquire about or join the register at
https://www.liverpoolwomens.nhs.uk/our-
services/donor-conceived-register-dcr/
Contact the Registrants group on
https://www.donorconceivedregister.
co.uk/

Surrogacy UK have created a Parents
Through Surrogacy group for members,
which provides social events and
workshops (including partnering with
DCN) so that children born through
surrogacy can meet with others and
parent can share experiences. https://
surrogacyuk.org/aboutus/membership-
benefits/

www.ingramcontent.com/pod-product-compliance
Lightning Source LLC
Chambersburg PA